Montessori Learning in the 21st Century

A GUIDE FOR PARENTS & TEACHERS

M. Shannon Helfrich

Foreword by
André Roberfroid

NEWSAGE PRESS
Troutdale, Oregon

MONTESSORI LEARNING IN THE 21ST CENTURY
A Guide for Parents & Teachers
Copyright © M. Shannon Helfrich 2011

First Edition Original Paperback
ISBN 978-0-939165-60-5

E-Book
ISBN 978-0-939165-61-2

NEWSAGE PRESS
PO Box 607
Troutdale, OR 97060-0607
503-695-2211
www.newsagepress.com

Cover and Book Design by Sherry Wachter
Printed in the United States

Distributed by Publishers Group West (Perseus)
www.pgw.com

Library of Congress Cataloging-in-Publication Data
Helfrich, M. Shannon, 1949-
  Montessori learning in the 21st century : a guide for parents and teachers / M. Shannon Helfrich ; foreword by Andre Roberfroid.
    p. cm.
  Summary: "A resource for teachers and parents interested in Montessori education and Dr. Maria Montessori's observations on child development. Discusses Montessori education and its viability in the 21st century. Explains the basic elements of child development through the lens of Montessori philosophy and neuroscientific findings"-- Provided by publisher.
  Includes bibliographical references and index.
  ISBN 978-0-939165-60-5 (pbk.) -- ISBN 978-0-939165-61-2 (ebook)
  1. Montessori method of education. I. Title.
  LB1029.M75H45 2011
  371.39'2--dc23
                                        2011030995

                        3 4 5 6 7 8 9

DEDICATION

*To Wilma, Margo
and Ann*

Acknowledgments

There are many who have influenced the writing of this first book and I wish to acknowledge those with special distinction:

Ann Wittmann, who inspired me with a passion to write as a young college student and who still inspires me today

Dr. Margaret Novak Brown, who introduced me to Montessori philosophy many years ago and started me down a lifelong path of wonder and discovery.

My mother, Wilma McDowall Helfrich, who inspires me to be my best and who has encouraged me to write with my head and my heart.

Many thanks to Maureen R. Michelson, my editor and publisher, who never lost faith that this book existed somewhere inside of me and who helped me find my writer's "voice." I credit her with helping me learn the true art of writing a book and then shepherding the book through its many stages to the end.

Thanks to Sherry Wachter for the excellent cover and book design. Her insights and expertise, especially with photos, have been invaluable.

Thanks to Gyles Fohl for creating the diagrams and images needed throughout this book.

Last but not least, I am grateful for all the teacher-education students and the children who have inspired me over the years. Every day, my interactions with these students reaffirm the importance of Montessori education no matter where I am in the world. Children are children unfolding in the same ways, following the same developmental patterns, manifesting the same needs.

Contents

FOREWORD

Why Montessori?

Since becoming president of the Association Montessori Internationale, many friends have asked me, "Why is a Montessori education a better way for our children?" Others have told me, "Education is facing a global crisis; why would an old method be an answer to a new problem?" Since I joined the Montessori movement in 2004, I have carefully considered these questions.

Of course, most Montessorians, parents and professionals alike, will have an answer to these questions. Many will say that surveys and studies prove the validity of the Montessori approach. Some will elaborate on the scientific evidence of a child's development; others will refer to their personal positive experiences with a Montessori education. All of these answers are true, but they are not enough to convince some of my friends.

When I read Shannon Helfrich's book, it became clear to me that, at last, I found the answer! Many books have been written about Montessori's method, this one is about *living* with it

This book is not a theoretical essay; instead, it is the story of a lifetime of experience by a loving mother who is a passionate Montessori teacher and a dedicated teacher trainer. This is the culmination of Shannon's learning, observing, reflecting, and practicing the Montessori approach to education for more than forty years. In addition, Shannon clearly has a deep respect for Maria Montessori, M.D., who was a brilliant and pioneering woman.

The most important message Shannon conveys in her book is the concern for the "discovery of the child." It is often said that Dr. Montessori discovered the child as a true, complete human being with her/his individual potential and capabilities. What Shannon explains is that Dr. Montessori did not tell us who or what the child is, but rather gave us an elaborate and effective method to discover the child ourselves. What Shannon offers parents and teachers is not just another book to learn from, but an invitation to observe and understand children—in fact, an opportunity to "discover" our own children.

For many years, Shannon has observed children in Montessori classes as well as Montessori teachers during their training. As a result, she has a deep understanding of Dr. Montessori's books and teachings, and an unequivocal confirmation that this educational approach is effective. Recent developments in neuroscience substantiate what Dr. Montessori observed and documented, and Shannon explains some of these fascinating findings about the brain and a child's development.

By watching carefully our children and using this book as a guide to observe intelligently what we see, every parent will understand the aspects of the Montessori environment, and the reasons why particular Montessori methods are used at particular times. The development of a human being from birth to adulthood is the result of different periods that correspond to a child's physical, intellectual, and emotional growth. Dr. Montessori called these periods the Four Planes of Childhood Development. Shannon walks her reader through each plane of development and explains how Montessori education supports a child's natural growth.

The guidance and assistance provided by the parents, along with the Montessori guides, must be in alignment with the natural development of the child's brain and body. This process follows specific periods that Maria Montessori called the "sensitive periods," which are contained within each plane of development. These sensitive periods correspond with a child's development of movement, language, sensory perceptions, and sense of order.

In addition, a child's brain is greatly influenced by interactions with the parents. When parents understand the different planes of development and the corresponding "sensitive periods," they can support their child as a Montessori student. Shannon explains how parents can participate and optimize the Montessori experience. Throughout the book Shannon emphasizes a very basic and essential element of the Montessori approach; it is a self-constructive process. As Shannon writes, "Parents have to learn to stand back and let their child figure out age-appropriate tasks. A child's experience must be hands-on and personal."

After reading this book, I found it striking to discover that Dr. Montessori's theories, Shannon Helfrich's lifelong observations, and neuroscientists' latest findings all contribute to a common understanding of the evolution of the human being. While it is true that during the early part of life a child's brain is mostly receiving and storing millions of bits of information, (Dr. Montessori called it "the absorbent mind"), a child also has to develop a capacity to classify, relate, and compare pieces of information. "It is not sufficient for the brain to simply take in information and to record it as separate and unrelated bytes of data," Shannon explains in *Montessori Learning in the 21st Century*. "There has to be a means for sorting and linking similar experiences and related data, resulting in the creation of intelligence." This book demonstrates how Montessori education facilitates the brain's development, a child's creativity, and evolving intelligence into young adulthood.

Several times throughout the book Shannon emphasizes the importance of a child's "self-construction," and her recommendation is to multiply opportunities for children to "do it themselves," especially during the early years. She writes, "For parents, the implications are that we must let our children be involved in the everyday tasks of life. Children have a strong desire to contribute, even though they are not as efficient or as skilled in their movement as older children or adults."

I was particularly fascinated with Shannon's explanation of why Dr. Montessori determined children like order in their lives. Children need a world "in order"; they want to make sense of things. Shannon notes, "Even a small infant is sensitive to the routine of the day. A certain comfort and security comes from the predictability of this routine." In fact, making sense of the world is the initial perception of a true sense of self and the beginning of independence.

In describing the sensitive periods, Shannon gives her reader access to the core of the Montessori method. Nothing in a Montessori classroom is happening by chance. Activities are the result of long and detailed observations, of in-depth analysis, and now, in the 21st century, supported by the latest scientific discoveries. But one must keep in mind that everything starts at home! It is therefore essential that the physical and emotional environment at home be consistent with the Montessori philosophy. Shannon offers clear and simple recommendations. "The purpose of the home environment is not childproofing, but child-preparing!" explains Shannon. " Spending time talking, singing, playing with your child is not just fun, it is actually productive work."

Throughout this book, Shannon offers many insights, stories, and simple explanations about how children grow and how Montessori education facilitates their development. In short, Shannon Helfrich invites us to take a fascinating journey, accompanying our child from birth to maturity from the perspective of the Montessori philosophy. Along the way, we discover the answer to my initial question: Why Montessori? The best answer to this question is not in theoretical debate, nor in surveys or reports. Shannon expresses it perfectly on the last page:

"Dr Montessori firmly believed that the child who experienced life in this manner during the formative period of life would seek out similar experience in later life. She believed that the child who grows and sees himself as a productive member of a positive society would grow into an adult who would desire a world that allows for similar experiences. This is the start of a global society based upon an inherent respect for all others, recognizing the commonalities of our humanity and the richness of our differences."

This is indeed *"the ultimate gift."*

—ANDRÉ ROBERFROID, President, AMI

Montessori Learning
in the
21st Century

CHAPTER ONE
The Century of the Child

Imagine the curtain of the twentieth century opening upon a stage. Gathered on this stage are many of the great minds of the world, poised to begin the mission of this new era declared the "Century of the Child." Among those great minds were Sigmund Freud, Karl Jung, Jean Piaget, Erik Erikson, Anna Freud, and a young woman named Maria Montessori. They would be among the early leaders of the new century guiding humanity to a greater understanding of the nature of the child, and creating a new vision for child development and education.

Over the next fifty years, these great thinkers performed key roles on the world stage that significantly influenced the dawning of a new reality for the twentieth century children—and beyond. Each of these individuals was a genius in his/her own right. Each contributed greatly, from a particular perspective, to the understanding of a child's nature regardless of race, class, or culture, and ultimately, to an understanding of our humanness. There has been no other time in history when so many great minds, all working simultaneously yet independently, escalated in such a dramatic way knowledge and understanding of the child.

At the dawn of the twentieth century, the child was a forgotten citizen. The common byword of the day in the Western world was "the child is to be seen, but not heard." Children were shuffled away; out of sight, out of mind, until such a moment when they were brought forth as proof of a parent's prowess and fertility. Children had no rights and were considered little more than small animals to be cared for and tolerated until the great moment when the "rational mind" appeared. The magical "age of reason" was thought to appear in the child somewhere around age seven. It was at this age, educational authorities determined a child's formal education could begin.

EARLY INSPIRATIONS FOR DR. MONTESSORI

While these influential thinkers turned their thoughts to life, learning, and the patterns of development, not one of them took up the cause of the young child more than Dr. Maria Montessori. In 1896, Maria Montessori became the first female to earn a medical degree in Italy, graduating with honors from the University of Rome Medical School. As a young physician, Dr. Montessori worked in the hospital wards, lectured at the University of Rome Medical School, and conducted research in the psychiatric clinic connected to the university.

It was through her research work on the development of the brain that Dr. Montessori first went to the local insane asylum looking for research subjects. At the beginning of the twentieth century, the only means to study the human brain was through research on subjects with abnormal brains. The best resource for subjects was the local insane asylum housing inmates ranging from the criminally insane to young children living in poverty who were labelled "misfits of society." At the insane asylum, children were housed alongside adults in a single institution. As a relatively new democratic nation, modern Italy did not have the resources to create separate institutions for those who needed to be removed from society and for young children imprisoned simply for trying to survive in a poverty-stricken environment. Thus, children were lumped in with adults in what was little more than a "friendly prison." It was here that Dr. Montessori first met children living under the direst of circumstances.

While research at the Orthophrenic Hospital was conducted on subjects of all ages, Dr. Montessori was particularly drawn to the conditions and circumstances of the children.

AMI Archives

Dr. Maria Montessori in 1909.

Dr. Montessori was horrified at the very thought of young children being housed with criminally insane adults. She was also mystified by the asylum staff's treatment of the children, many of whom considered the children little more than unmanageable animals.

One particular day, Dr. Montessori arrived just as the children were finishing lunch. She witnessed the children scrambling on the floor in search of fallen crumbs of bread. The caregivers at the asylum interpreted this behaviour as evidence that the children were little more than animals. However, Dr. Montessori viewed this behaviour as that of stimulus-starved children. The asylum was devoid of toys, educational materials, or even the simplest items of everyday life. The stark nature of this environment left the children limited to the most mundane sources of intellectual stimulation.

Dr. Montessori witnessed the children's great curiosity and intensity even as they explored the breadcrumbs. Her heart went out to these impoverished children living in such a sensory deprived environment and it became her mission to save as many of them as she could.

First, Dr. Montessori pleaded with the staff for the separation of the children from the asylum's population of primarily insane criminals. She also took advantage of the fact that the research subjects she chose would be removed from the insane asylum and taken into residency at the Orthophrenic Hospital. Dr. Montessori found herself adding more and more children to the list of research subjects in an attempt to get them out of the insane asylum.

While her research and that of her colleagues revolved around the medical aspects of treatment, Dr. Montessori was drawn to the children's strong desire to learn. She realized early on that the surrounding environment must play a role in supporting and nurturing a child's development. She was drawn to researching the potential of these children.

Dr. Montessori gave a great deal of thought and energy toward understanding the anthropological dynamics of the abnormal child. She also recognized how important it was for children to have decent hygiene and a healthier diet. As a part of her research, she began to chart the physical development of the children as their overall health began to improve. At the same time, Dr. Montessori became increasingly curious about the learning potential of these disadvantaged children. She believed they had innate powers that could be tapped into, even when there appeared on the surface to be little potential still remaining in these so called "mentally defective" children.

THE WRITINGS OF ITARD AND SÉGUIN

Dr. Montessori began researching academic writings regarding instructional techniques that might be used with the children from the asylum. She found little, aside from the writings of two French medical doctors from the 1800s, Jean Marc Gaspard Itard and Edouard Séguin. Both of these men had worked with children labelled as "mentally defective."

Dr. Itard became a surgeon and worked in the army during the French Revolution in the 1790s. In 1796, Dr. Itard was working as a surgeon in the hospital at Toulon, France. He showed great talent and was later accepted for an internship in Paris. In 1800, Itard became the chief physician for the National Institute for the Deaf and Mute in Paris. Around this same time, a "wild boy" was discovered in the forest near Aveyron, France. He was thought to be about twelve years old, mute, and walked on all fours at the time he was discovered.

Many of Dr. Itard's contemporaries considered this boy to be nothing more than an abandoned, mentally retarded child. However, Dr. Itard believed the boy had simply been isolated from human contact for too long. He worked with the Wild Boy of Aveyron, later named Victor, for five years. He believed he could teach Victor through stimulation of the senses and adaptation to social norms.

Dr. Itard had only limited success in his work with Victor. However, he was later awarded for his work as one of the earliest teachers advocating for special teaching methods to educate disabled children. Today, Dr. Itard is hailed as the "father of special education." His writings formed the basis for the work of Edouard Séguin, who also did some of the earliest work with mentally retarded children.

Dr. Séguin came from a family of prominent physicians and received the best medical training that existed in the early nineteenth century. Interested in psychology, he studied under Dr. Itard who was instrumental in directing Dr. Séguin's interests toward the needs of mentally retarded children.

In 1837, Dr. Séguin began to work with his first mentally retarded patient. He began with stimulation of the senses, following in the footsteps of his mentor. He firmly believed that mental deficiency was not a matter of an abnormal brain but of an abnormal "nervous system."

Dr. Séguin's class of mentally retarded patients grew rapidly. He focused on the development of instructional activities that would serve to stimulate the individual sense organs as the portals to the mind. Sensory training and motor training with age appropriate activities were key components in working with the impaired students. Dr. Séguin applied these techniques and provided a rich, stimulating environment for his subjects. He also created educational guidelines that involved intellectual and physical tasks specifically to help disabled students develop independence and self-reliance.

Dr. Séguin's educational guidelines influenced later work by others educating children with special needs. Sadly, despite his accomplishments, in many ways Dr. Séguin considered himself a failure since he could not find a cure for mental deficiency.

The writings of these two doctors inspired Dr. Montessori. She also realized they were the only documented practical attempts to teach children with mental deficiencies. Dr. Montessori went to Paris and translated these writings word-for-word by herself so she would not miss any nuance of inspiration. While both Drs. Itard and Séguin felt they were unsuccessful in many aspects of their work, both developed important techniques for working with disadvantaged children. Dr. Montessori recognized the tremendous value in their educational approaches.

Montessori teachers today will recognize the influences of Dr. Itard in the use of the moveable alphabet and of Dr. Séguin, in the matching of pairs material in the sensorial area—tasting bottles, sound boxes, color tablets. These techniques and the learning materials described in their writings served as Dr. Montessori's beginning point.

DR. MONTESSORI CREATES HER OWN PROGRAM

Her lectures at various medical and educational congresses, especially the Educational Convention in Turin in 1898, led to greater prominence. Italy's Minister of Education appointed Dr. Montessori as the Director of the Orthophrenic School, a new medical-pedagogical institute in Rome. In this position, Dr.Montessori gave lectures to teachers on learning abilities and appropriate techniques for teaching children with learning difficulties.

For two years, Dr. Montessori trained teachers to use the techniques she had developed. Oftentimes, she was in the classroom working with the children as much as the teachers she was training. During this exciting time of developing her program, Dr. Montessori believed these teaching techniques would be appropriate and beneficial for all children. However, she also faced the scorn of her colleagues. Many of Dr. Montessori's medical contemporaries accused her of lowering herself to the level of a kindergarten teacher. This criticism did not deter Dr. Montessori from her research and application of a new approach to teaching children.

Dr. Montessori's initial work with children who had been labelled "defective and hopeless" was so successful that many of these children passed the state examination that "normal" children took in the public schools. Many educators wondered what magical instructional techniques Dr. Montessori had discovered that made it possible for her "defective" students to excel beyond the "normal" students. At the same time, Dr. Montessori wondered about the limitations of Italy's state educational system.

In 1904, Dr. Montessori gave up her direct work with the children at the Orthophrenic School, resigned from all hospital obligations, and closed her private medical practice. She chose to again become a student at the University of Rome. This time, she studied philosophy and anthropology. She also continued to lecture at the University about her experiences working with children at the Orthophrenic School.

THE FIRST CHILDREN'S HOUSES

In 1906, Dr. Montessori was offered the opportunity to create a series of schools for infants in the tenements of Rome. A group of wealthy bankers, calling themselves the *Instituto Romano di Beni Stabili* (Roman Good Building Institute) was revitalizing abandoned housing complexes. In the late 1800s, there were sections of Rome that had large housing complexes partially built but never finished due to a series of economic recessions.

This group of bankers bought the abandoned buildings and refurbished them to provide housing for people from the countryside moving to the city to work in factories. At the time, these tenements were considered a great example of urban renewal. The bankers were quite proud of their efforts and were determined to do the same in several other parts of Rome.

The first housing area refurbished was the San Lorenzo quarter, a very poor neighborhood within Rome. Workers who lived in these buildings considered them a great improvement over their previous living situations. The bankers got great positive press coverage for their successful efforts. There was only one problem; San Lorenzo was "infested" with a gang of young children who were left to their own devices while their parents were at work. The children were vandalizing the buildings and creating mischief.

The Director of the Roman Association for Good Building asked Dr. Montessori to take charge of these wayward children who ranged in age from two to seven years on a type of "home school" setting. The owners gave Dr. Montessori one apartment for her needs, but not much more. She opened the first of these "infant schools" in the San Lorenzo quarter on January 6, 1907, which is the Feast of the Epiphany, a special Christian celebration.

Dr. Montessori called each of her schools *Casa dei Bambini*, or as we know them today in Montessori education, Children's Houses. Dr. Montessori opened two Children's Houses in the tenements. The remainder of her schools were opened in other venues throughout Rome and later Milan because of a growing

Helfrich Photo Collection

The original Casa dei Bambini *in Italy as it looked
one hundred years later in 2007.*

enthusiasm for her successful approach to teaching children. A series of sixteen schools was to become the foundation and the catalyst for a great social and educational experiment.

The opening of *Casa dei Bambinis* in Rome and Milan allowed Dr. Montessori a variety of children from diverse backgrounds to become part of the experiment. For example, she opened a Montessori school at the British Embassy for the education of the staff children. The Catholic Franciscan Sisters opened a Montessori school specifically for children orphaned by the 1908 Messina, Sicily earthquake that killed some 70,000 people. From this point on, Dr. Montessori dedicated herself to a deeper understanding of the nature of learning in children.

DR. MONTESSORI'S TRAVELS TO THE UNITED STATES

In 1911, Alexander Graham Bell (the inventor of the telephone) read about Dr. Montessori's teaching methods in "McClure's," an American literary and political magazine. The magazine had featured a series of articles by Josephine Tozier that described Dr. Montessori's work as "this marvellous new educational approach." Bell offered to help Dr. Montessori get to the United States to lecture about her findings because of the growing interest in her educational approaches. Samuel McClure, editor and owner of "McClure's," saw the opportunity to spread the word through a speaking tour and the creation of a Montessori Department in his magazine, which would offer ongoing information on Dr. Montessori's work. In 1913, Dr. Montessori made her first visit to the United States, sponsored by Samuel McClure. She travelled and lectured throughout the United States and was a huge success.

Dr. Montessori returned to the United States for a second—and last—visit in 1915 to help set up a Montessori classroom exhibit at the Panama-Pacific International Exposition, also called the World's Expo, in San Francisco. When Dr. Montessori arrived at the venue she quickly saw the challenge of setting up a model classroom in an open space. She wanted to protect the children and still give the visitors a close-up view of what was happening inside. Dr. Montessori resolved this challenge by having a series of glass walls erected around the open space. Bleacher seats were provided outside the glass walls for the observers and visitors. This "glass classroom" soon became a favorite stopping place at the World Expo.

Thousands of parents applied for their children to be accepted into the model classroom at the World Expo, but only thirty children were chosen. Dr. Montessori allowed the classroom sessions to be conducted by two of her American teaching students. A favorite time for visitors was just about lunch time when they could watch the children prepare their own food, then serve each other with great elegance. Visitors were mesmerized with how the children conducted themselves with great grace and dignity. The Montessori exhibit was awarded both of the gold medals for Education at the close of the 1915 World Expo.

Montessori Approach Expands Worldwide

Despite prejudices and discouraging articles written against the Montessori approach, and the advent of two world wars, Dr. Montessori's work continued to grow in influence and application throughout the world. Dr. Montessori spent the remainder of her life exploring the means to educating "man" to his fullest potential. She wrote prolifically about her discoveries and trained teachers worldwide who used her methods.

Dr. Montessori never considered herself an educator, but always saw herself as a researcher. The children were her subjects and from them she learned everything she needed to know to meet their needs. She did not believe that her discoveries were ever hers, but that they belonged to the children. Indeed, it was not her method, but rather the children's method since they were the authors who revealed their natural way of learning to her.

Despite Dr. Montessori's humility in taking credit for her work, she interpreted what she observed in the children's learning. Her interpretation of these observations and the creation of activities for the children was truly Dr. Montessori's genius. She learned much from her study of Drs. Itard and Séguin's writings and findings. She also expanded her understanding by sharing ideas with her contemporaries. However, it was Dr. Montessori's insight that gave structure to the application of the ideas and the creation of a teaching or "pedagogical system" for early childhood education.

Dr. Montessori eventually expanded her exploration of the learning needs of children to include six-to-twelve-year-old students, young adolescents, and the young adult. She saw the need for a specific type of environment and a particular set of learning activities and techniques appropriate for the development of the full human, or what she called "the new man." Today in Montessori, we think of this as the development of "the new human." Dr. Montessori saw early learning as the process of creating the whole of the new personality of the individual. In essence, each child is creating the core of the man or woman he/ she will become in the years that follow.

Dr. Montessori survived two major world wars, the second of which could have easily destroyed her life's work. She became increasingly convinced that the only way to change society was through the education of the young child. She believed that children with a strong positive sense of self, and a respectful positive attitude toward others, could become the basis for a new society. Dr. Montessori envisioned this new society based on cohesion, respect, and dignity. It would be a society grounded in peace, not war.

Throughout her lifetime, Dr. Montessori was quite vocal in her message regarding the nature of peace and the role of education. Her efforts were recognized with nominations for the Nobel Peace Prize in both 1949 and 1950.

Dr. Montessori's legacy exists today through the organization, the *Association Montessori Internationale* (AMI), which she created with her son, Mario Montessori. Today, her legacy is carried out in AMI training centers throughout the world and in all classrooms where teachers still apply Dr. Montessori's original principles in the twenty-first century.

CHAPTER TWO

The Relevance of Montessori in Modern Times

The question begs to be asked: Can Dr. Montessori's ideas—first formulated more than one hundred years ago—still be effective in working with children today? The answer is unquestionably, Yes!

In essential ways, the child today is the same as the child of yesterday and the child of tomorrow. Dr. Montessori used her keen powers of observation to study the nature of the child across many cultures, but she never had the technology to verify her theories. Today's researchers have the benefits of a myriad of scientific methods for measuring learning in children. The modern challenge and delight is to combine the power of technology with the power of observation. In many ways, current brain research offers an analytical explanation of Dr. Montessori's insights and theories in much the same way that scientific tools available today confirm Albert Einstein's theories.

One might think it strange to explore educational theory (pedagogy) through neuroscience, but Dr. Montessori actually began her professional career studying the brain. Dr. Montessori's theory of child development provides specific aspects and observations that today can be examined in the light of current neuroscience. It is exciting to consider Dr. Montessori's finding through the lens of modern science, and to confirm what she realized through years of working with children, regardless of sociological circumstances or culture.

Understanding what Dr. Montessori learned about children's development and ways of learning, now confirmed scientifically, will help educators and parents alike. This enlightening information will help deepen parents' and teachers' understanding of how their daily interactions impact children.

DR. MONTESSORI'S FINDINGS AND CURRENT BRAIN RESEARCH

Montessori teachers and parents, often called "Montessorians," might consider it a current fad or a novel approach to look at Dr. Montessori's philosophy of child development through the lens of brain research. However, a revisit to Dr. Montessori's own writings reveals that we are simply picking up the study where she left off.

As a Montessorian for nearly forty years, I have always believed that the study of the brain and what we call intelligence can deepen our understanding of child development and provide greater insight into the basic needs of children. One cannot read far into Dr. Montessori's works without getting a sense that this was important to her as well. A couple of years ago, I had the opportunity to read a rare first edition of Dr. Montessori's first book, *The Pedagogical Anthropology*, which we had just purchased for the library at the Montessori Institute Northwest where I was working at that time. When I gingerly opened the book Dr. Montessori wrote in 1913, it was with delight and affirmation that my eyes fell upon several early diagrams of the brain. Her diagrams reflect some of the earliest understandings of the nature of the human brain.

Dr. Montessori's work at the Orthophrenic School in Rome was a systematic study of the nature of the brain. For instance, she took cranial measurements of children's heads as they grew, which reflected changes in the brain. Early brain studies held the hypothesis that race and possibly culture influenced the size

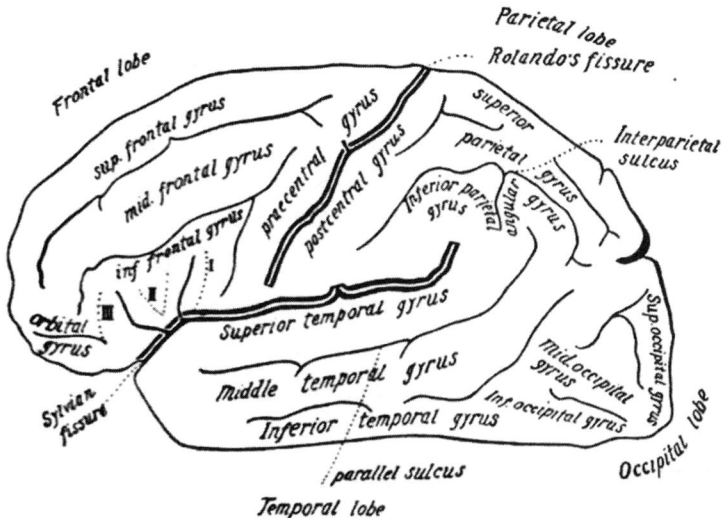

Brain diagram from "Pedagogical Anthropology"
(Helfrich Photo Collection)

of a human brain. Dr. Montessori wanted to explore the idea that good health and living conditions were a greater factor than genetics or cultural exposure. I believe Dr. Montessori created these drawings during her earlier cadaver studies in medical school.

When we put Dr. Montessori's brain study into the context of the early twentieth century, we can see the inherent limitations. There was no way to really study a living human brain without breeching the cranial cavity. Simple characteristics associated with brain density or assumptions regarding parts of the brain used for specific functions could only be explored with cadavers' brains. And yet, the scientists of Dr. Montessori's day were intensely interested in the knowledge and insight that brain research could provide for understanding human beings.

Dr. Montessori soon shifted her focus from looking at cranial measurements to looking at children whom she could observe in their everyday lives. From these observations, she made many incredible interpretations of what was happening in a child's brain.

One common criticism about Dr. Montessori's observations and findings is that she did not clinically document her theories about the nature of the child's mind. Dr. Montessori understood that the technology required to accomplish a so-called "proof" did not exist in her lifetime. However, Dr. Montessori did write extensively regarding her discoveries and empirical understanding of the brain. Her book, *The Pedagogical Anthropology*, was exclusively about her studies of the human brain. In this book, she wrote prolifically about her theories on the nature of child development, and in particular, the nature of a child's developing mind.

Today, we have the advanced technology to study the brain in action as humans at all phases of development participate in numerous life activities. Amazingly, Dr. Montessori's theory on childhood development holds up under the scrutiny of modern neuroscience.

In June 1996, a group of prominent educators and neuroscientists met in Chicago to correlate all the current brain research. Participants exchanged many points of view for two days at the symposium and published a paper titled, "Brain Development on Young Children: New Frontiers in Research, Policy and Practice." Educational researcher and writer, Rima Shore, took these findings and additional information extracted from the neuroscientists' presentations and summarized them in her book, *Rethinking the Brain: New Insights into Early Development*, published in 1997.

Shore noted that neuroscientists at the symposium acknowledged that as recently as the 1970s they still believed the structure of the brain was already genetically set at birth. Up until that time, neuroscientists tended to underestimate the importance of a child's early life experiences and their impact on brain development. Neuroscientists also did not recognize that a child was an active participant in his or her brain development. However, at the 1996 symposium, the neuroscientists presented information that dramatically shifted science's view of brain development in young children. They enthusiastically acknowledged the influences of early childhood development and the child's role in his/her brain development. This was an astounding and crucial admission on the neuroscientists' part. Even more powerful was the concluding statement by this eminent panel of scientists and educators who wrote:

> Indeed, brain research is one of the most exciting and fruitful scientific endeavors of the last decades of the 20th century. But unless this research finds its way into our homes and health clinics, our early childhood centers and classrooms, America's schools and human service institutions will remain locked in a 19th-century paradigm.[1]

NEW UNDERSTANDINGS OF CHILDHOOD LEARNING

As the neuroscientists and educators looked at the implications of current research, they arrived at five significant conclusions regarding early childhood learning. If we look at the five conclusions reached by the neuroscientists and examine them in light of Dr. Montessori's writings, there are striking parallels between what Dr. Montessori observed one hundred years ago and what neuroscientists are confirming today.

The following are the five major discoveries documented by the neuroscientists at the 1996 conference regarding the brain as referenced in Rethinking the Brain. When I read these neuroscientists' five basic conclusions, I was astounded and thrilled. As a Montessori teacher and trainer who passionately believes in Montessori's theory on childhood development, this scientific proof confirmed Dr. Montessori's empirical findings.

Let's look at each of these conclusions in light of Dr. Montessori's writings.

CONCLUSION ONE: **"How a brain develops hinges on a complex interplay between the genes you are born with and the experiences you have."**[2]

In *Rethinking the Brain*, Shore notes the neuroscientists' new findings: "The brain is affected by environmental conditions, including the kind of nourishment, care, surroundings and stimulations an individual receives. The impact of the environment is dramatic and specific, not merely influencing the general direction of development, but actually affecting how the intricate circuitry of the human brain is 'wired.'"[3]

In Dr. Montessori's book, *Spontaneous Activity in Education*, her empirical findings were in line with what neuroscientists found. She wrote: "Intelligence...is the sum of those reflex and associative or reproductive activities which enable the mind to construct itself, putting it into relation with the environment."[4]

Furthermore, in Dr. Montessori's book, *The Absorbent Mind*, she explained: "The child has an intelligence which is not conscious though it often seems to be endowed with reason. It begins with knowledge of his surroundings. This is an intense and specialized sensitiveness in consequence of which the things about him awaken so much interest and so much enthusiasm that they become incorporated into his very existence. The child absorbs these impressions not with his mind but with his life itself."[5]

Dr. Montessori observed that a child's needs cannot be met adequately by any hereditary pattern, but must be guided by other influences that enable a child to become a unique individual who belongs to the specific culture or society into which he is born and raised. The language created by the child, the aspects of coordinated movement, and the understanding of social norms and taboos—none of these could possibly be hard wired into the brain. In fact, we know that the brain is not even fully developed physically at birth. Almost all the brain cells needed throughout life are present at birth, but these cells are immature at best. The brain will grow in density as it creates new dendrites (extensions of nerve cells) and synaptic connections.

CONCLUSION TWO: "Early experiences have a decisive impact on the architecture of the brain, and on the nature and extent of adult capacities."[6]

The neuroscientists and educators at the symposium stated, "The brain has a unique way of developing that sets it apart from every other organ in the human body. Gradually creating and organizing billions of brain cells in a predetermined manner during early childhood would demand more information (in the form of genetic coding) than the body could possibly dedicate to this purpose. Nature solved this problem by evolving a more economical system."[7]

It is important to note the tremendous, ongoing brain activity in infants and toddlers and how this is reflected in the creation of synaptic connections. The developing brain produces billions of neurons and synaptic connections, many times more than it will eventually need. In the early years of life, the brain development of infants and toddlers proceeds at a staggering pace with approximately 100 billion neurons creating synaptic connections within the first three years of life. Each neuron has the capacity for up to 100,000 synapses through its dendrites.

By the age of three years, a child's brain has built 100 trillion synapses.[8] This would be an overwhelming system to bring into some semblance of organization. So the brain begins to organize itself by linking cells stimulated by the same event or stimulus. The more times the event occurs or the stimulus is taken in, the more connections are made. This process also allows cells that do not receive further stimulation to be discarded (or unlinked) from the system. These cells contain superfluous, unrelated information and are irrelevant as part of a singular piece of learning. The brain begins to search out patterns of similarity as a means of simplifying the organizational schematic.

The growth of dendrites and synaptic connections in the brain is not enough for the child's development within the first three years of life. A parallel aspect in brain development is the growth of the brain's cerebellum, which will grow dramatically for a short period of time shortly after birth and again between six-and-fifteen months of age. (Brain development and maturation are discussed in Chapter Four.)

Dr. Montessori recognized the importance of a child's exposure to and relationship with the environment as the stimulus for brain development. She wrote in her book, *The Formation of Man*: "If the child, from birth onwards, has to create his personality at the expense of his environment, he must be brought into contact with the world...he ought to take part in it...to be in touch with the life of adults. If he is to adapt himself to the environment, he ought to take part in the public life and to be a witness to the customs which characterize his race."[9]

Later in her life, Dr. Montessori wrote: "The child absorbs knowledge directly into his psychic life...a kind of mental chemistry goes on within him..the child undergoes a transformation. Impressions do not merely enter his mind: they form it...the child created his own 'mental muscles, ' using for this what he finds in the world around him."[10]

Interestingly, scientists also make an important connection between the physical development and maturation of the brain and the child's relationship with the primary caregiver. In *Rethinking the Brain*, the neuroscientists stated: "A strong, secure attachment to a nurturing caregiver also appears to have a protective biological function...'immunizing' the infant to some degree against the adverse effects of stress and trauma."[11]

Neuroscientists have confirmed that children learn in the context of important relationships. The best way to help very young children grow into curious, confident, able learners is to give them warm, consistent care so they can form secure attachments to those who care for them. Children who receive consistent responsive care in the first years of life are more likely to develop strong social skills. In his book, *The Biology of Transcendence,* Joseph Chilton Pearce quotes Lena Allen-Shore, Ph.D., founder of The Center for the Advancement of Human Potential in Philadelphia, Pennsylvania, stating: "Interactions with the mother directly influence the growth and assembly of the brain's structural systems that perform self-regulatory functions in the child...and mediate the individual's inter-personal and intra-personal processes for life."[12]

Dr. Montessori and her contemporary, Erik H. Erikson, a developmental psychologist who also studied Montessori education, recognized the importance of the child bonding with a primary caregiver—who, in those times was always identified as the mother. Dr. Montessori viewed this relationship between child and mother as the most important relationship in a child's life. In today's society, we can expand the reference to "mother" to also include any committed and nurturing primary caregiver.

Dr. Montessori noted that first and foremost, a primary relationship is essential to the child's early survival, and later, strongly influences the child's confidence in exploring the surrounding environment. She believed that if the child felt secure in the presence of her mother [or primary caregiver], then the child was more likely to take greater risks exploring the environment. Erikson went so far as to declare that a child's experience in bonding with the mother in the first twelve months of life would forever impact a child's capacity for trust and mutuality.[13]

CONCLUSION THREE: **"Early interactions don't just create a context; they directly affect the way the brain is 'wired.'"**[14]

In *Rethinking the Brain,* Shore reported the neuroscientists' findings regarding a timeline for brain development as quite different from what science traditionally believed—a belief that Dr. Montessori worked to change. The neuroscientists stated, "The brain's intricate circuitry is not formed at a steady pace; rather, it proceeds in waves, with different parts of the brain becoming active 'construction sites' at different times and with different degrees of intensity."[15]

The notion that brain development follows a set time line for the acquisition of certain skills and abilities is not a new idea. The recognition of prime times for learning has been around for many years. Whether they are called prime times, critical periods, windows of opportunity, or sensitive periods, they are all the same.

Montessorians and other early childhood educators readily recognize that a child seems to learn certain skills and abilities spontaneously during certain periods of development. Once these windows close or the sensitive period passes, the learning requires a much greater conscious effort and is never as optimally integrated into the child's developing personality.

For instance, children's brains between birth and age six years are completely open to learning and integrating into their lives any language they are exposed to. During this sensitive period for language, a child can easily become bilingual (or more) and speak the language(s) without an accent. However, as adults, learning a second or third language requires much more focus and effort. I studied both Spanish and German as a young adult, but I never really *learned* either language, and I have not retained what I learned. Now in the sixth decade of my life, I am studying Mandarin Chinese with some hope of a slightly better result. However, I fully accept that I will never speak Mandarin as well or as confidently as a native speaker.

Dr. Montessori recognized this phenomenon in the writings of Dr. Jean Itard, who worked with the wild boy, Victor. Dr. Itard reflected on his constant struggle to humanize Victor. Even simple tasks like eating with proper utensils and speaking in clear sentences were impossible tasks. Victor's life in the forest, isolated from human society at a very young age, left Victor unable to create a clear spoken language. While he was able to master a small, limited vocabulary and to even recognize some of these words in written form, Victor was never able to formulate thought or to communicate with complete sentences reflecting thought. The window of opportunity, or sensitive period for language, which ends around the age of six, was over by the time Victor was exposed to spoken and symbolic language. Victor's limited capacity for learning language reflected the struggle of a child who had missed this important sensitive period.

In more recent times, we have the circumstances of the Romanian orphans who did not walk or talk when they were rescued in the 1990s. These children had been kept in isolated crib-like enclosures with little or no contact with each other or with their caregivers. This left them with little exposure to spoken language. The children were fed enough to keep them alive but little more. They had no motivation to stand and all their movement was greatly limited by the size of the crib in which each child lived. Harry T. Chugani, M.D., at the University of Michigan, Ann Arbor, spent several years working with Romanian children and their adoptive families, trying to help the children overcome the limitations of learning to walk and talk far beyond nature's timeline.

In an article first published for the Association for Research in International Adoption, Dr. Chugani wrote: "The major finding in this study was that a substantial proportion (46 percent) of globally intact children who have experienced severe deprivation exhibit persistent functionally relevant impairments in one or more specific cognitive domains. The domains most often affected were executive functioning, language, and memory with 41 percent of the globally intact children evidencing problems in at least one of these domains. This is the first report of impairment in performance on a measure of sustained attention in children with such histories. Impairments in language, memory, and executive functioning are likely to have important consequences for adjustment to academic and social environments."[16]

Dr. Montessori recognized early along in her work that there were patterns of interest for children and resultant learning that appeared and disappeared at predictable intervals during child development. In her book, *The Secret of Childhood*, Dr. Montessori wrote: "Children pass through definite periods in which they reveal psychic aptitudes and possibilities which afterward disappear. That is why, at particular epochs of their life, they reveal an intense and extraordinary interest in certain objects and exercises, which one might look for in vain at a later age."[17]

CONCLUSION FOUR: **"Brain development is non-linear: there are prime times for acquiring different kinds of knowledge and skills."**[18]

In *Rethinking the Brain*, Shore wrote: "Scientists have learned that different regions of the cortex increase in size when they are exposed to stimulating conditions and that the longer the exposure, the more they grow. While learning continues throughout the life cycle, there are prime times for optimal development—periods during which the brain is particularly efficient at specific types of learning. These periods are described as 'critical periods' or 'plastic periods.'"[19]

Neuroscientists have also come to understand that once the prime time has passed, opportunities for forging certain kinds of neural pathways appear to diminish substantially. This concept is built on the premise that development depends on the exposure of the brain to many kinds of stimulation according to a predictable timetable.

When there is a disruption of the normal developmental schedule of experience, neural connections are not made properly, and the cortical columns (a group of neurons in the brain cortex) that result are thinner than they should be. During developmental "prime times," neurons can create synapses most easily and efficiently.[20]

In Dr. Montessori's theory of child development, these periods have traditionally been referred to as "sensitive periods."

The discovery of these powerful periods of intense interest and activity became the key to Dr. Montessori's creation of an educational approach. With a poetic flare, she described these sensitive periods in *The Secret of Childhood*: "When some of these psychic passions die away, other flames are kindled and so infancy passes from conquest to conquest; in a continuous vital vibrancy, which we have called its joy and simplicity. It is through this lovely flame that burns without consuming that the work of creating the mental world of man takes place."[21]

CONCLUSION FIVE: "By the time children reach age three, their brains are twice as active as those of adults. Activity levels drop during adolescence."[22]

The neuroscientists' final conclusion as reported in *Rethinking the Brain* is that the first three years of life seem to set the foundation for all development that follows. If this is the time when the brain is most active in creating synaptic connections, then parents and educators must be sensitive to the first three years of a child's life as the foundation upon which all further learning is built. It seems strange to say, or believe, that the potential for logical thinking, for planning, and for all later skill training is founded upon the neurological pathways built in the first three years of life.

The implications here are that a child must be assisted and supported in this early stage of development, for it will impact the remainder of her life. Since the 1990s, there has been a great push to refine the educational approach for children in Montessori settings before the age of three years. Infant communities are quickly becoming a significant part of the continuum of Montessori offerings.

Dr. Montessori wrote in *The Absorbent Mind*, "Man possesses creative sensitivities instead of hereditary models of behavior, and if it is due to these that adaptation occurs to his surroundings, then it is clear that the whole psychic life of the individual stands upon a foundation which must be laid down by them in the earliest years."[23]

Some might interpret this as a fatalistic point of view if a child's early needs are not met. Indeed, it is important for parents and educators to pay close attention to the developmental needs of the child in these first three years of life. However, recent research does show that early intervention between the ages of three and six years can result in great improvements for the child deprived of early developmental stimulation. Even some of the less abused Romanian children were able to learn and function quite ably with intervention.

Children are quite adaptable through age six years and even through age twelve years. It is during this time that the child can work to overcome many of the limitations due to the lack of early stimulation. It doesn't mean development is as easy as it would have been early on, but a child can "mend" many of the dropped stitches of development with active intervention.

For example, today, there are many children who benefit greatly from occupational therapy in order to overcome lack of coordination. Children with sensory integration problems are helped greatly by therapies specifically geared to their distinct problems. Some children suffer from over sensitive stimulation and some children have the opposite problem with under-achieving stimulation. Occupational and physical therapies help children learn how to cope and train the brain to better balance the sensory data coming in.

There is certainly much more to explore and understand about the nature of intelligence and this wonderful organ, the brain. We will delve into some of these implications in much greater depth in the following chapters.

THE ESSENCE OF THE CHILD

The Montessori tradition in education stems from Dr. Montessori's work in the late nineteenth and early twentieth centuries. As long as the essence of the child remains the same, the essence of a Montessori approach to education will be the same. Only minor changes in methodology and approach have occurred over the many years since Dr. Montessori's death on May 6, 1952.

The Montessori approach is based on the natural, spontaneous development of the child. A common guiding phrase among Montessori teachers and parents is "Follow the Child." As long as the nature of the child unfolds in the same manner from generation to generation, the child's developmental needs and the resultant learning will stay constant.

Dr. Montessori offers educators today the same insights into the nature of the child that she observed one hundred years ago. Montessori teachers bear witness to these same developmental phenomena everyday in their work with children. To bring the Montessori approach into the twenty-first century does not require that we change or invalidate the Montessori tradition. However, it does require that we look to current knowledge to better understand the nature of the child. This is no different from what Dr. Montessori did. She took the work of Drs. Itard and Séguin and integrated their findings with her own findings. By doing so, we continue the great tradition she modeled so wisely.

CHAPTER THREE

The Big Picture of Child Development

Understanding developmental stages of children is essential. Every aspect of a child's development leads to the creation of him or her as a unique human being. A child's foundation is established in the early years of life, and this development continues throughout adulthood. Indeed, a child's development builds from one platform to the next in a connected continuum, much like scaffolding from one stage to the next.

Often, developmental theorists begin with this image of the whole child and then proceed to define the individual stages that make up the whole. Dr. Montessori began her work with infants and young children, and later expanded her work to include school age children, adolescents, and young adults.

During the early stages of her career, Dr. Montessori was constantly on the move, travelling from one place to another, lecturing, visiting schools, and training teachers. When she had to spend extended time in India during World War II, she finally took the time to consolidate her lifetime of observations and research. At the time, Dr. Montessori was sixty-nine years old and she had planned to stay in India only six months. She ended up living in India for six years until the end of the War in 1945. During this time, she began to develop a complete overview of a child's development as a continuum from birth through age twenty-four.

Toward the end of her life, Dr. Montessori created two schematics of her theory of childhood development in stages, along with an educational plan. Dr. Montessori wrote a pamphlet called, "Four Planes of Education," which looks at a child's life as a series of developmental stages, building one upon the other.

A stage theory plan for explaining childhood development was not unique to Dr. Montessori. This same approach was shared by a number of her contemporaries. Sigmund Freud created a stage theory of development based upon the psychosexual aspects of development. Erik Erikson followed with his theory, "Eight Ages of Man," based on the psychosocial aspects of development. Jean Piaget, the first president of the Swiss Montessori Society, created his stages of development with a cognitive base. In modern times, theorists continue to use stage theory. For example, twentieth-century American psychologist Lawrence Kohlberg identified stages of moral development.

While stage theory makes many significant contributions to the understanding of growth and development, like all theories, it has strengths and weaknesses. Stage theory presents a neat chronology, often with ages affixed for different aspects of human development. Different age stages may serve as an appropriate guideline indicating shifts or changes in development, but they do not give much flexibility for the timing of the development of an individual human being. For instance, one infant may begin taking her first steps or saying her first words at six months, while another infant may wait until a year or more.

Another potential weakness of stage theory is the concept that each stage is influenced by the developmental work accomplished in the preceding stages. This would not be a limitation if a child's development could progress with few obstacles and within a beneficial learning environment. However, often that is not the case. A difficult home life, family financial strains, medical problems, or unrest within a community or country can all be realities that inhibit a child's healthy development. Later on, learning can be impacted by unfinished or underdeveloped skills from a previous stage. Clinical psychology as we know it today is based upon the reality of "unfinished" developmental work.

This is not a fatalistic point of view, but an acknowledgment that skills and abilities build over an extended period of time. For example, Dr. Montessori and modern neuroscientists identified the relationship of the infant with a primary caregiver as a profound influence on a child's brain development. This significant relationship also has a profound social effect because this is when an infant first learns to trust another human being. The positive influence of this first bonded relationship is key to a child being able to connect in a positive manner with other beings throughout life. This primary relationship will impact his ability to feel comfortable making new friends at age seven. It will influence a child's ability to create a significant relationship in adolescence or to weather the challenges of marriage as an adult. This is not to say that a child is doomed for life if he does not have a strong bond with a primary caregiver early in life, but it does indicate that this could be a struggle later in life.

Dr. Montessori based her stage theory on observations of children throughout the world in natural settings. The diversity of children in different cultures, with different languages, and varying socio-economic conditions, allowed Dr. Montessori to develop a picture of universal patterns for all children.

Dr. Montessori's stages of development. (AMI Archives)

The Four Planes

These are the stages or planes of childhood development that Dr. Montessori identified:

- 0-6 years: Infancy
- 6-12 years: Childhood
- 12-18 years: Adolescence
- 18-24 years: Maturity

Each plane encompasses six years of growth and development. Within each plane there are two phases. For example, the first three years are the period of greatest change, a period of creation. The second phase in the First Plane is followed by a three-year period of integration or crystallization. Dr. Montessori observed that the new characteristics in each phase that a child absorbs present themselves early in each new plane.

However, it is not sufficient for these new characteristics to just be present in a child; instead, the child must fully integrate the new characteristics into her psyche, so that the characteristics are deep-seated and accessible for future learning. These characteristics cannot be a mere overlaying of new information, but must be solidly woven into the fabric of the child's personality. That is why it is important for a child to have a period of time to practice and refine skills, gain new knowledge and understanding, and adapt new attitudes and aptitudes before relying on these new capacities to function fully in life.

For example, consider the development of movement. Early in the First Plane of development, at about one year old, the infant begins to walk upright and over the next two years masters the art of upright, bipedal movement. Just being able to walk upright is not a sufficient level of motor development as a child must also be able to use her motor skills to carry out everyday activities in a coordinated or integrated manner. Indeed, the child must become the master of movement.

In the crystallization phase of the First Plane, from ages three to six years, the child needs many opportunities to practice purposeful movement, eventually mastering graceful, coordinated movement. If we carry this example one step further, in the Second Plane the young child's legs grow longer. Early on, the young person struggles to re-shape coordination to accommodate her longer legs. Once the young person is comfortable with this new level of coordination she strives to apply coordinated movement in the context of games and sports. This enhances the level of coordination and allows the young person to learn how to move in concert with others, whether playing games, dancing, or working together.

In the Third Plane of development, the young adolescent must master coordination once again as her body goes through its final great physical changes. Each new level of coordinated movement becomes the springboard for the next challenge. Having time and opportunity to solidify each new level of coordination is a luxury afforded by nature and this is reflected in the period of crystallization at the end of each plane.

DEFINING ASPECTS OF EACH PLANE

Through her observations, Dr. Montessori concluded that there were several defining aspects of each plane of development. Each of these would be significant in establishing and recognizing the needs of a growing child and the optimal environment needed to support him or her. These defining aspects can be summarized as follows:

- Recognition of the innate learning powers naturally present in the child.
- Recognition of the kinds of activity that support and nurture development spontaneously.
- The surrounding environment has the flexibility to change and accommodate the different skills and activities needed in each plane of a child's development.

A child's changes from one stage to the next resemble a metamorphosis—a child's version of the caterpillar becoming a butterfly. Psychologists and physicians from Dr. Montessori's time to our current day recognize that each child's growth and development is irregular in the importance or impact that each stage has on a child's personality. While following the stages described in Dr. Montessori's schematic, one has only to watch a child in one's own family to know this truth. Dr. Montessori understood this and created a second chart called "The Bulb," which first appeared on a chart dated 1951.

THE FOUR PLANES OF DEVELOPMENT

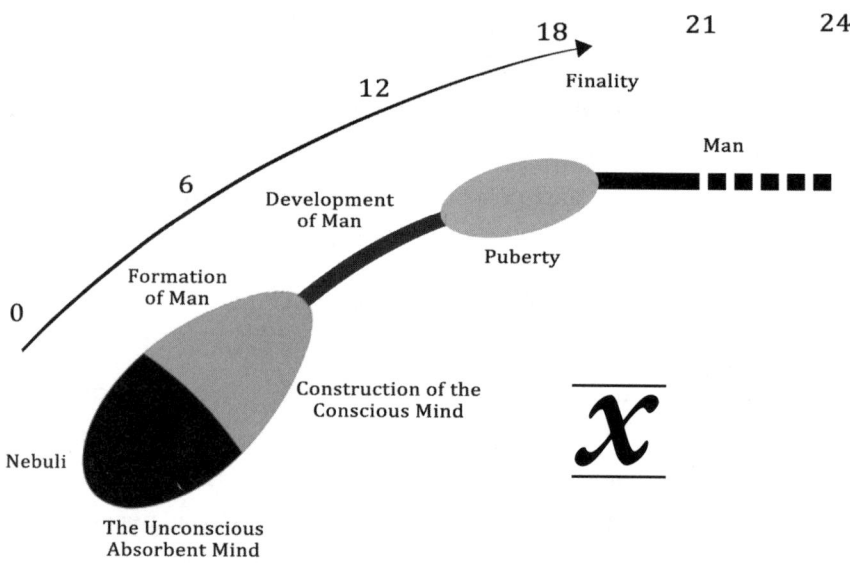

Dr. Montessori's bulb chart reflects a more realistic picture of growth and development in children.

THE BULB CHART

Dr. Montessori's bulb chart reflects a more realistic picture of growth and development in children. There is a dramatic period of growth from birth to six years. There is no other time in the life of a human when growth is greater or more influential for later life.

The blackness at the beginning of the bulb represents an extended period of "unconscious" development. Unconscious does not equate with "comatose" or a lack of significant brain activity. Instead, this is a period when a new human absorbs all that the world offers without the need or ability to filter this information or consciously process it. A young child's brain would not have the capacity to discern what information is important, essential, or significant. So a child takes in all that he is exposed to and stores this stimuli in his brain for future reference. This phase coincides with the second and third conclusions neuroscientists determined from their research, which I explained in Chapter Two:

- "Early experiences have a decisive impact on the architecture of the brain, and on the nature and extent of adult capacities."
- "Early interactions don't just create a context; they directly affect the way the brain is 'wired.'"

The next portion of the bulb chart Dr. Montessori colored a fiery red to indicate the dramatic learning that unfolds in a young child, usually 3 to 6 years old. The rate of a child's growth and learning witnessed in this plane will never again be matched in any other plane of childhood development.

The long narrow section representing the "Development of Man" (about 6 to 12 years), Dr. Montessori colored a verdant green to indicate constant growth. This time period is important for developing the individual psyche, but growth that is not dramatic. During this time, a child develops significant new capacities, skills, and aptitudes created from the experiences of the Second Plane. Again, there are innate powers and resulting creations specific to this plane. For example, during this time a child will create an understanding of right and wrong, which then provides a foundation for the creation of a personal ethics.

When the First and Second Planes are taken together developmentally, the work during these two phases results in the creation of a unique individual human being. In essence, the developmental work in the Second Plane (6 to 12 years) is the completion of the developmental work begun in the First Plane (birth to 6 years).

In the Third Plane of development (12 to 18 years), Dr. Montessori's bulb chart returns to a fiery stage represented by the color orange. The Third Plane is like a second birth—the birth of the social being. During adolescence, the young person again undergoes a dramatic physical and psychological shift leading to a new role in life. The dramatic physical changes of puberty result in a state of physical instability. During this time, an adolescent is prone to illness, and the psychological changes result in dramatic mood swings and emotional instability.

Unfortunately, most parents and educators have difficulties understanding adolescents. If only parents and teachers could celebrate the tremendous social preparation that is occurring during the Third Plane, adolescence might not seem so overwhelming. With a better appreciation of the critical developmental plan of adolescence, adults could be more adept at understanding and meeting the needs of their growing child as an emerging social being. The adolescent is truly the most misunderstood and criticized being in today's society! The current educational approaches used in most developed countries are more at odds with children and their needs during this stage of development than with any other plane of development.

The developmental work of the Third Plane is completed in the Fourth Plane (18-24 years) as the young adult prepares to take his place in society. During this time, young adults are now ready to carry out their task of contributing to the society they are a part of. By the end of the Fourth Plane, young adults are in tune with themselves, sensitive to the surrounding world, and prepared to start a new family unit—provided they have had the opportunities and support to develop through the previous three planes. At this point, a child has grown to manhood or womanhood and will participate in the nurturing and perpetuation of the human family.

The "X" sign at the bottom right of the bulb chart was Dr. Montessori's way of indicating that learning would continue and the person would continue to change, but that the role of formal education was generally concluded. This does not minimize the importance of graduate school or advanced education, but reflects the typical standard of Dr. Montessori's day when traditional education was generally completed by age twenty-four and the young adult entered society as a contributing member.

Dr. Montessori intentionally chose to forego laboratory research and/or documentation of her theory because she wanted to focus on the practical applications of her theory. She believed strongly that her insights on child development would be wasted if she did not create the basis for a new educational approach. In 1937, Dr. Montessori presented a lecture to the Association for the Reform of Secondary Schools and the Dutch Montessori Society in Utrecht, The Netherlands. In that talk, Dr. Montessori urged her colleagues: "We have to take a new path. We must give everything that is necessary to develop the personality to the highest possible degree, taking as a basis the human powers themselves, unknown in their greatness and beauty, which are shown by youth."[1]

Exploring the Educational Planes

An exploration of each plane of education focuses on three aspects:

- The unique learning powers present during that particular period.
- The learning outcomes that result.
- How a natural occurring environment can support and sustain a child's learning and development.

FIRST PLANE: BIRTH TO SIX YEARS		
MOTIVATING POWERS	OUTCOMES/ CREATIONS:	PREPARED ENVIRONMENT
Absorbent Mind Sensitive Periods	· Spoken Language · Coordinated movement *(locomotion and the hand)* · Will *(intentionality)* · Capacity to Make Choices · Independence · Capacity as a sensorial learner · Capacity for obedience · Orderly mind · Mental schematic for understanding the world · Love of learning · Capacity to love and connect with others	**0-3:** · A stable home environment with a primary care giver · Interesting objects to explore · Age appropriate, purposeful activities · A secure yard, outings with the family · Routines **3-6:** *All of the above, plus:* · The opportunity to be with other similar aged children · Specific activities that stimulate and support development

This First Plane sets the foundation. We can look at the outcomes/creations and see the fundamental pieces of development. It is these skills and abilities that the child is going to build upon throughout the next three planes. The most important role of the parents during this First Plane is to provide a loving, nurturing home environment.

Parents can also help by providing their child with experiences that expose the richness of the world that surrounds them. For example, an infant is curious about every object that surrounds her. Babies are driven to touch and taste all that comes within their reach. Parents can offer many interesting and safe objects for their children to explore.

Of course, this desire to explore is accompanied by a drive to move. Just watch a child beginning to crawl. This child will wiggle and squirm any time she is wrapped tight, held, or strapped into the car seat. In the early years of the First Plane, the home environment is the child's primary world. They want to "get into things." A reachable cupboard in the kitchen with pots and pans and other interesting objects can engage a child for a long time.

By the age of 18-24 months, the young child loves to be outdoors and explore nature. A child is fascinated by the fuzziness of a caterpillar, the smell of a rose, or the every move of an animal or bird. A child loves to take long walks along the riverbank or to run with happy feet across a field of prairie grass. A child's world is rich only if she is free to really explore that world. Parents must be patient and trusting as their child explores, gets dirty, makes mistakes, and practices, practices, practices new movements and skills. Often, adults will view a young child's repetitive activity as inefficient and time-consuming processes.

For example, picture a child just learning to button his own coat. It seems to take forever, and the coat may not be perfectly aligned or have every button done up, but the look of delight on the child's face once she is finished is worth the wait. Another example is most children love to help in the kitchen while dinner is being prepared. Something as simple as preparing a salad can be rich and satisfying for a child. The lettuce leaves may not be uniform and the carrot slices will be of interesting shapes and sizes, but the opportunity to participate in family life, to contribute, and to practice her newfound skill is priceless.

It is also essential for parents to recognize that their child must conduct this self-constructive process for herself. Parents have to learn to stand back and let their child figure out age-appropriate tasks. Again, this will require large doses of parental patience. A child's experience must be hands-on and personal. A child's home environment must be supportive of independent activity and opportunities for the child to make choices.

Children have a strong desire to live as meaningful members of the family, which is their first social community. Even something as simple as bringing the infant to the table while the rest of the family is eating dinner helps the baby to feel accepted. The baby can feel the energy of the family dynamic and observe the patterns of interaction happening before her eyes.

Parents can nurture their child's growth by providing some choices, whether at the dinner table or when dressing in the morning. A young child who is allowed to choose which clothes to wear and to dress herself, or choose from mealtime offerings what and how much food to eat, begins to build a positive sense of self-esteem and a feeling of competency. If your child has a difficult time deciding what to wear, try giving her a choice between "the red shirt or the blue shirt." Sometimes, exercising a choice between two items is a learning experience in itself!

In the later years of the First Plane, when a school-age child begins to understand the symbols of her culture's written language (reading and writing), she feels comfortable in a society where symbolic language surrounds her. A child who can practice the grace and courtesies of human interactions quickly feels secure and comfortable around others.

From the security of the home environment, a young child in the Second Plane of development now begins to explore the larger world surrounding him. Home provides the secure launching pad for venturing out into the world.

The powers of the mind allow a child to explore elements of life beyond the present moment. In the Second Plane, young students

SECOND PLANE: SIX TO TWELVE YEARS		
MOTIVATING POWERS	OUTCOMES/ CREATIONS:	PREPARED ENVIRONMENT
Powers of Abstraction Power of Imagination Points of Consciousness	• Uses writing and reading for research and authorship. • Understanding of time and passage of time. • Ability to work with a team. • Experience with division of labour. • Creates code of ethics. • Sense of justice, fairness. • Expanded vision of the world and how it works. • Sense of confidence in self. • Intellectual independence.	• A secure home base and family unit. • A diverse world to explore. • Opportunities to explore. • Outings into the world. • Classroom for research and in-depth analysis of data. • A peer group. • Heroes or models.

(age 6 to 12 years) are fascinated with history and what life was like long ago. This interest serves as the vehicle for expanding their skills of reading and writing. Now, a child discovers the delights of working with peers. While working with other children, a child begins to recognize the strengths and limitations of his skills and begins to offer his developed skills to the task at hand.

In the Second Plane, a child experiments with the diverse roles of teamwork and division of labour. The child's natural tendency to create a "club" comes to the fore, so children can explore not only the roles of teamwork, but also the value of rules and issues of fairness. Dr. Montessori's approach was to view the real "work" of a game to be the children sorting out and coalescing all the various interpretations of the rules of the game. Actually playing the game, or winning and losing, was not important to the children or judged as significant by Dr. Montessori. She saw the "real work" taking place before the children began to play the game, and these experiences serve as the foundation for the development of a personal code of ethics.

During this phase, children determine what is innately right or wrong when they make judgments. At this stage of development, a child becomes very rigid in the interpretation of rules, often seeing only a black or white version. Security comes from this rigidity, and the ability to apply the rules offers the experience needed to see beyond the obvious.

It is also during the Second Plane that a child is drawn to heroes and role models he can emulate. This is an expression of the child now aware of becoming a social being. Whether the hero is a music star, a top athlete, or a comic book super power, matters little. All of these hero images serve the same purpose—someone who has developed powers beyond the child's!

Parents can serve as good role models provided they live by the same standards and values that they teach. A child who sees his parents reading and enjoying the discovery of new ideas through a good book, witnesses another way to explore the world.

Parents who allow their children to participate in family life and their community, allow their children to feel connected. This is a good time for parents to assign simple chores so their child can experience responsibility. All the functional independence children develop during the First Plane they can now use to contribute to the life of the family. Whether washing the dishes, raking leaves, planting in the garden, feeding the dog, or putting their things away, children experience being a part of a community. Children realize they have a role in order to make all the parts succeed.

Parents can support their child's desire to explore the world and allow him to explore on his own within safe limits. At this stage, a young child's tricycle has now morphed into an older child's two-wheeled bicycle. There is no way we can keep children confined to their single block in the neighbourhood when an interesting world awaits discovery.

The child who has always relished doing things with the family, now stretches his wings and wants to stay overnight with a friend or go to the zoo without Mom and Dad. Parents can take heart from the moments when home and family once again become the safe haven. Children in the Second Plane of development are delighted to share new discoveries and new insights with someone who will listen. They need to sort out the mechanics of logical thinking and judgment by practicing. Children love to have a long conversation or to conduct an "interview" to learn more about someone they find interesting.

At the end of the Second Plane, we see children who are strong physically, confident in what they know, and knowledgeable in how to get information they are still curious about. We see human beings who are fully developed as individuals with the personal and intellectual skills to take on society.

THIRD PLANE: TWELVE TO EIGHTEEN YEARS

From the confident, secure human being of the Second Plane comes the adolescent and the Third Plane (age twelve to eighteen). Adolescence is a tumultuous time in child development, representing a second period of dramatic change. Adolescents face major changes physically, both internally and externally. Indeed, when they look in the mirror, they often don't recognize the face staring back. Even parents are astonished with the physical changes, sometimes looking at their growing child quizzically in the morning, wondering if they grew in the night. In fact, researchers have documented that children can lengthen up to a quarter-of-an-inch in the course of one night's sleep!

THIRD PLANE: TWELVE TO EIGHTEEN YEARS		
MOTIVATING POWERS	OUTCOMES/ CREATIONS:	PREPARED ENVIRONMENT
Hormones of puberty. Human Tendencies.	• A capacity to form and sustain relationships. • Sense of self as a member of society. • Emotional and economic independence. • A love of the earth and a personal connection to it. • Morality (*ivory tower thinking*).	• Loving adults who enjoy adolescents. • A place in the country for work and exploration. • A creative arts shop, places for contemplation. • Machines and tools. • A family as a base to re-connect with. • Opportunities to work in the professional world. • Exploration of many occupations.

The physical changes are significant enough, but coupled with the emotional changes, this is a time when a young person is prone to illness and in need of the greatest support that can be given. Intellectual pursuits now take second place to the exploration of human relationships. Nine-year-old children who perceived the opposite sex as disgusting, now, as adolescents, see them in a new light. What was disgusting is now cute or at least tolerable. During puberty, the body releases hormones that cause physical changes and emotional changes. Puberty is the last great physical change needed to complete all the powers of the body, including reproduction. The thickening of the vocal cords, the elongating of the torso, and the maturation of the sexual organs all are signs of this great change in the Third Plane.

The body also begins to signal its attraction to its own species. Adolescents are very preoccupied with their own attractiveness and usually acutely aware if others are noticing them. The safety of the social group is a starting point, but quickly the adolescent begins to explore exclusive relationships. Adults reflecting on their own development may recognize that they still have friendships that began during this time in life.

Because of the great changes and the anguish this can cause, adolescents need time and space for contemplation, reflection, and meditation. Often, parents perceive adolescents' desire for alone time as a form of isolation or disrespect for the family and its needs. Parents often perceive their child slamming a door shut as an insult when actually it is just a plea for quiet alone time.

In addition, adolescents need avenues for self-expression, whether it is music, art, writing, acting, or sports. These are the necessary emotional outlets that an adolescent uses to release excess energies and emotions. Parents can support, understand, and be patient with their children in the Third Plane. They can also be heartened by the fact that their adolescent children still come to talk with them, albeit on the adolescent's terms, and only when she is ready. The greatest attributes a parent can offer an adolescent are being available, and being a quiet listener. Lecturing the adolescent rarely works!

The needs for movement are reflected differently in this phase of the young person's development. First, the body has to master a new level of coordination as it stretches to almost its full adult size. Parents might remember their own feelings of awkwardness when they were adolescents and tripped over the "invisible" crease in the living room carpet or the raised edge of the sidewalk. Fortunately, it doesn't take long for the adolescent body to once again find its physical equilibrium.

45

Adolescents may continue to participate in sports as an outlet for energy and for the social dynamic. On another level, adolescents seek opportunities to travel without their parents. They want to know they can "make it" in the larger world independently, exploring far-flung places they have only read about, and applying all their functional skills to taking care of themselves. This is a time when students participate in extended class trips, or other adult-supervised group activities that do not include lots of parents.

Dr. Montessori explains the Third Plane as a time when adolescents are sorting out the possibilities for contributing to society. They love to explore different kinds of professions and different interests, and how these might be applied to real jobs. Adolescents need to know they have worth as individuals independent from their parents.

Understanding economics and how the world works are now fascinating in this phase of development. Adolescents need to find ways to become a part of the world economy. For some, this will be a first paying job, for others it will be creating a cottage industry. An adolescent's desire to earn money and begin to be self-sufficient is coupled with a sensitivity to the needs of others. Some of the most compassionate and altruistic human beings are adolescents. They will serve in the local soup kitchen to feed the hungry or volunteer to help handicapped children. Adolescents can be faithful companions to senior citizens—all with no expectation for pay, just happy to know they can help someone in need.

In the Third Plane, the adolescent is usually interested in learning to drive a car, provided the family has the means to offer this privilege. As scary as this seems to parents, the young adult who has been responsible in other tasks applies that same responsibility to this new rite of passage. This is a time when parents must trust that all the precursor experiences are in place! This is a demanding time for parents in learning to let go, and practice discernment with their child who is in a full-blown metamorphosis into adulthood.

FOURTH PLANE: EIGHTEEN TO TWENTY-FOUR YEARS		
MOTIVATING POWERS	OUTCOMES/ CREATIONS:	PREPARED ENVIRONMENT
Specific Studies to prepare for a specific profession. Human Tendencies.	• A worker who functions for altruistic and economic purposes. • Balance of power drives. • Capacity for intimate relationship (commitment) and the responsibilities of a new family unit.	• Specific occupational knowledge and skill opportunities. • The world. • Family and friends.

Dr. Montessori's Fourth Plane, ages eighteen to twenty-four years, describes the finishing touches in a child's development. At this plane, the young adult begins to visualize how he can best apply what he knows to meaningful work in society. This is also a time to determine what skills he wants to develop further.

Young adults establish economic independence and ideally begin to participate as full citizens in their community and country. By this age, young adults have a strong sense of self and their relationship to the world as they launch their generation's full participation both locally and globally. Maintaining balance is the key for young adults in the Fourth Plane as they complete their education for a chosen profession. Each young adult has to find his or her unique balance, finding a place between the power drives of society and the altruistic efforts for the sake of those less fortunate.

As young adults take their place at the table of life, they accept the responsibility to create a new family unit or to nurture the next generation in meaningful ways that may not directly involve parenting. The cycle begins again. Not everyone chooses to marry and create a new family, but most will seek ways to serve humanity in positive ways.

Each of Dr. Montessori's planes gives great insight into how a child or young adult can best be assisted in meeting developmental challenges. Dr. Montessori's findings are the basis for children's development and provide a solid foundation for education—if education is going to help children toward their optimal fulfillment.

Dr. Montessori's empirical findings, supported by modern science's findings, call for educators to place greater emphasis on early education as the foundation for all later learning. Fortunately, in the past ten years a growing number of educators worldwide have recognized the importance of early education and have implemented many of the educational programs Dr. Montessori developed nearly a century ago.

CHAPTER FOUR
The Child's Mind

If the ultimate goal of a child's "self-construction" (human development) is to become a thriving young adult with the skills and attributes of a fully evolved human, then we must make sure that the foundation is solid and strong. Dr. Montessori understood that the least understood plane of development was the First Plane. In large part, this is because the young child appears so limited in capacity and is usually not considered to display any great intelligence.

It is only in recent decades that infants and young toddlers have been recognized for their tremendous intelligence and capacity to learn. When cultures and societies disregard their young children's intelligence, this is dangerous. It is also unfair to the children who are, in reality, great intelligences trapped inside the limitations of physical bodies they cannot yet control.

In the past, adults' condescending attitude toward the young was common. I have often questioned, "Why is it possible to look at a young child and fail to see intelligence?" What Dr. Montessori recognized, and current neuro-scientific evidence confirms, is that infants and young children are incredibly intelligent—just not in the ways adults generally think of as intelligent.

WHAT IS INTELLIGENCE?

Defining intelligence is a challenging task. Common English dictionaries offer four key ways to think about intelligence:

- Intelligence is the ability to learn or understand from experience.
- Intelligence is the ability to acquire and retain knowledge.
- Intelligence is the ability to respond quickly and successfully to new situations.
- Intelligence is the ability to use reason in problem solving and directing one's conduct effectively.

It is interesting that these definitions imply that intelligence is more than just a capacity within the brain. Instead, intelligence is manifested in developed abilities that are then applied to everyday life.

In 1921, writers at the *Journal of Educational Psychology* asked fourteen renowned psychologists to define "intelligence." While their responses varied, there were two common elements:

- Intelligence is the capacity to learn from experience.
- Intelligence is the ability to adapt to the surrounding environment.

Once again, we see that intelligent people view intelligence as more than just knowledge recorded and organized in the brain. Intelligence is also the ability to use acquired knowledge for one's own purposes in response to life's challenges.

Dr. Montessori shared this view of intelligence and observed it for many years in infants and young children. In her own writings, she noted that intelligence is "considered the sum of those reflex and associative or reproductive activities which enable the mind to construct itself, putting it into relation with the environment."[1] Dr. Montessori saw this manifested in the quickness with which the brain can function. She wrote:

> To be rapid in reacting to stimulus, in the association of ideas, in the capacity of formulating a judgment- this is the most obvious manifestation of intelligence.
> This "quickness" is certainly related to the capacity for receiving impressions from the environment, elaborating images and externalizing the internal results.[2]

Dr. Montessori was, herself, quick to acknowledge that this speed of responsiveness had to be learned. The sensory apparatus is fully in place at the time of birth, but it needs a period of maturation. While most of the sense organs are fully functional when a child is born—with the exception of the cones and rods of the eyes—it is the brain that has to be "trained" to recognize and process the stimuli it receives.

While gathering sensory data is one of the mind's tasks, the real work of intelligence is in making *distinctions* in the interpretation of this data. On this point, Dr. Montessori wrote:

> To be able to distinguish is the characteristic sign of intelligence: to distinguish is to arrange. Order is, in short, the true key to rapidity of reaction.[3]
> ...The consciousness may possess a rich and varied content; but when there is mental confusion, the intelligence does not appear[4]....to be able to distinguish, classify and catalogue external things on the basis of a secure order already established in the mind—this is at once intelligence and culture.[5]

Jacob Bronowski, Ph.D., an acclaimed author as well as a mathematician, scientist and philosopher, wrote about intelligence in his book, *Origins of Knowledge and Imagination.* Dr. Bronowski's perceptions of the brain and intelligence were similar to Dr. Montessori's. He wrote, "...this kind of discrimination can be achieved because the system of interconnectedness is such that a great deal of overlap is created, and as a result not only the brain, but the eye itself makes inferences about the world."[6]

Intelligence, no matter how we define it, relates to the preparation of the brain and its capacity to carry out its requisite functions in an effective and efficient manner.

DEVELOPMENT OF A CHILD'S BRAIN

A child's mind is a mystery to both the child and to most adults. The only thing known for sure is that a child's mind works differently than the rational, adult mind. Dr. Montessori chose to label the child's mind as the *absorbent mind.* In her writings, she described how an infant/child's mind takes in all the sensorial and emotional data present in the environment without filtering or prioritizing. A child's absorbent mind takes in the totality of the impressions and records them directly into the unconscious mind. These impressions are recorded in the neurological networks and become available for later learning. A quick look at the neurological aspects of the brain helps to enlighten our understanding of just how this happens.

At birth, the brain contains trillions of brain cells awaiting activation. This is not to imply that no learning has occurred in the womb, but that there has been limited stimulation up to this point. In fact, there is evidence of intelligent activity in a fetus as early as three to four months when the brain stem is active and the brain cells are moving throughout the brain in readiness for specific activities.[7]

At birth, the human brain has virtually all the cells it will need throughout a person's whole life, but most of these cells are considered "immature cells."

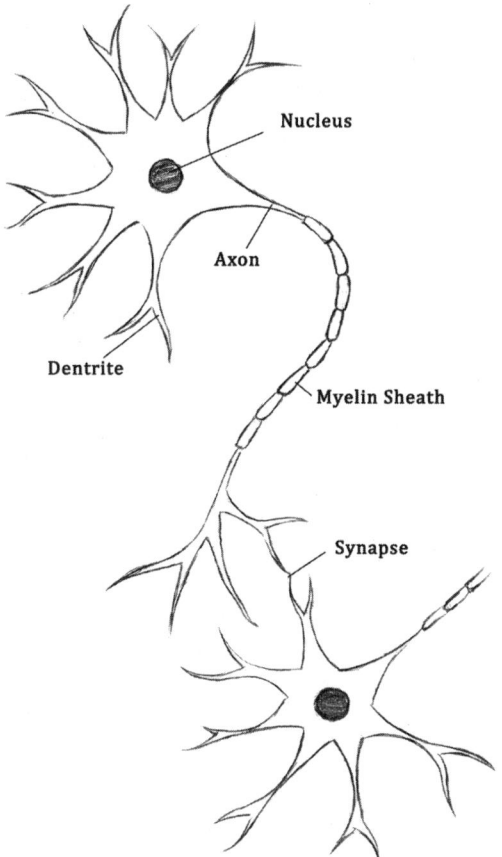

Diagram of brain cells and the myelin sheath.

An immature cell has a nucleus with several dendrites around the nucleus that are responsible for receiving energy, which is transmitting data to the cell. An immature cell also has an axon, a usually long nerve fiber that generally conducts energy (data) away from the cell to receptors in other cells throughout the body. The axons in immature cells have very few dendrites.

As a child's senses take in data, they transmit the information to the neural cells, which creates a chemical and electrical reaction. Upon activation, the cell nucleus generates additional dendrites and the axon begins to generate a coating of myelin, a fatty substance that covers and protects nerves. This tissue sheathes the axons, which protects the axons and assures the passage of electrical and chemical stimuli in a specifically defined pathway. This process is called myelinization or myelination.

Myelinization is analogous to the plastic coating over the exterior of an electrical cord. If you come into contact with a frayed cord, you experience electrical energy travelling where it was not intended. The shock is painful and certainly not a motivation for further interaction! In the same way, the brain needs the electrical and chemical energy to flow where it is intended in order to create specific neural pathways. Frayed nerve endings and inefficient pathways clog the thinking and responding process. The myelin sheathing then protects the flow of energy and allows for definition of efficient usable pathways.

Myelinization begins at the base of the neck. Simultaneously, it can move in different directions. It moves down the spinal column and influences the development of movement, or it moves up into the brain from the base of the stem toward the frontal lobe. As an infant grows, you can see the effect of myelinization down the spinal cord, which promotes the capacity for movement in a newborn. Clear indicators of myelinization in a baby include lifting the head and shoulders, sitting unassisted, and pulling himself upright. Through all of these progressive movements, the body is coordinating the muscles as the neural cells get accurate and efficient messages from the brain. This downward process of myelinization is virtually completed by about fifteen months of age.

However, myelinization upward from the brain stem toward the frontal lobe is a much more lengthy process. Evidence suggests that the totality of the process may only be completed when a young person is about fifteen years old. You may have had the experience of conversing with a teenager who looks at you with rapt attention and says, "I never thought of it that way before." We might attribute this statement to new experience on the part of the teenager, but more aptly, this statement reflects the fact that neural cells in the pre-frontal cortex have become myelin-ized and can now make connections that were not previously possible.

Another example of upward myelinization can be observed in a young child around eighteen months old who begins to learn and use many new words daily. This child is making connections between the neural cells in the left hemisphere of the brain with neural cells in the right hemisphere.

SYNAPTIC CONNECTIONS AND BRAIN GROWTH

As the cells mature, the brain's density increases. This den-sity is the result of dendrite growth and synaptic connections building between dendrites. Dr. Montessori spoke of the ability of a child's mind to incarnate knowledge. In E.M. Standing's book, *Maria Montessori: Her Life and Work,* the author quotes Dr. Montessori as saying, "It is logical that if the psychic life is to construct itself, by incarnating the environment, the intelligence must observe and study it first."[8]

The term "incarnating" might seem strange to use in refer-ence to the development of a young child's mind, but when you look at the nature of the brain cells, you see how this is pos-sible.[9] As individual brain cells are stimulated, electrical and chemical energy moves through the cells resulting in the growth of dendrites. Each dendrite that exists within a cell is capable of connecting with a dendrite from another cell. In essence, each stimulated cell is building itself and expanding its inherent capacities. This means the brain is literally creating itself and its knowledge from the absorbed experiences.

When the energy within a cell passes through the end of a dendrite, it creates a "synapse," which is a force field between two dendrites. As the energy passes from the dendrite of one cell to that of another, the energy leaps this space and a connection is made. The more a cell is stimulated, the stronger the connection because more synaptic connections are created.

Learning is the result of these synaptic connections. Over time, the brain builds neural pathways; a series of connections that link associated impressions. As the experiences of a child increase, the brain is able to refine and simplify these connections, making the related information accessible to the conscious mind. Brain development, from here on, is a process of pruning and reorganizing as the brain selectively eliminates excess synapses and organizes remaining synapses to be more efficient. As a child grows, an overabundance of connections gives way to a complex, powerful system of neural pathways.

The brain knows which connections to keep and which to discard according to the stimulation the synapses receive. When some kind of stimulus activates a neural pathway, all the synapses that form that pathway receive and store a chemical signal. Repeated activation increases the strength of that signal. When the signal reaches a threshold level, the synapse becomes exempt from elimination and retains its protected status into adulthood.

The Cerebellum as the Command Center

One other aspect of brain development necessary for the fullest integration and organization of information is the cerebellum. In *The Absorbent Mind,* Dr. Montessori described the development of the cerebellum as one of the essential physiological keys in development.

At birth and throughout the first six months of life, because the cerebellum is so small, other folds of the brain cover it. Then, between six and fifteen months of age, the cerebellum goes through a period of tremendous growth.

This allows the cerebellum to now function as the command center for the rest of the brain functions.

The cerebellum controls the reticular formation, which is a diffuse network of nerve fibers and cells in parts of the brainstem that are important for regulating consciousness or wakefulness. The cerebellum also controls the flow of the impulses of the

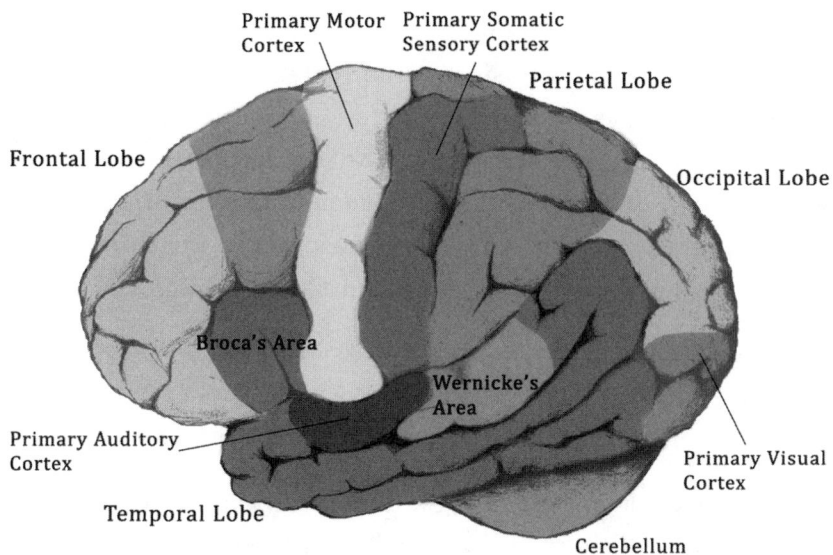

Primary Motor Cortex
Primary Somatic Sensory Cortex
Parietal Lobe
Frontal Lobe
Occipital Lobe
Broca's Area
Wernicke's Area
Primary Auditory Cortex
Primary Visual Cortex
Temporal Lobe
Cerebellum

brain and the powers of concentration and attention. It serves to focus the energies flowing into the synaptic connections. This energy flow is critical in fine-tuning the creation of the neural networks and for strengthening the synaptic connections.

The role of the cerebellum both in early childhood, and again, in early adolescence, has been well documented in modern times. In a 2008 "New York Times" article entitled "Play," the renowned play psychiatrist and founder of The National Institute for Play, Stuart Brown, M.D., talked about the cerebellum as it relates to play. He said, "...the cerebellum needs the whole body movements of play to achieve its ultimate configuration."[10]

Play, activity, and movements with focus result in stimulation for the cerebellum. A child needs this activity for the release of chemicals in the brain that serve the cerebellum. It is not enough for the biological process to unfold without this extra stimulation. Again, we see the interplay between our biological nature and the nurture provided by the environment.

Renowned child-development specialist and author, Joseph Chilton Pearce, writes about the cerebellum extensively, describing it as "made of extensions of all three brains in our triune system, and [it] is involved in just about everything we do...."[11] The term "triune system" refers to what has traditionally been recognized as the reptilian brain, the mammalian brain, and the neo-mammalian brain. These three aspects of the human brain have evolved over the whole of our human existence and all three aspects still control various responses to life.

THE ADAPTABILITY OF THE BRAIN

The brain has a unique way of developing that sets it apart from every other organ in the human body. It gradually creates and organizes billions of brain cells in a predetermined manner during early childhood. This would be an overwhelming task if all the information were to be contained in the genetic coding.

While it might seem nice to think that genetic coding could serve as a protection against cultural and parental influences that are not positive, this would also result in a limited capacity for the human brain to adapt to changing conditions. All humans would end up behaving exactly the same in response to life situations. There would be no capacity for individuality and free will.

The brain's capacity to make changes and to adapt to specific circumstances is defined as the "plasticity of the brain." Helen Neville, Ph.D., is a neuroscientist and the director of the Brain Development Lab at the University of Oregon. For years, she has studied the plasticity of the brain in creating the systems upon which intelligence are built. Her findings show that the brain's systems are created through experiences with the external environment, yet these systems are not hardwired into the brain and can be developed in different parts of the brain if there is an obstacle or limitation. For example, the visual cortex of a blind person can be used for processing auditory or language information. This plasticity allows the brain great flexibility in creating all the systems needed to function in life. While this plasticity is greatest in the young child, there are strong indications that the brain retains this flexibility throughout life.[12]

Dr. Montessori wrote at length about the importance of the absorbent mind at work. Gathering sensory information from the environment stimulates the brain cells. The chemicals stimulate connections between similar bits of information. Gradually, the network becomes more complex and integrated.

It would be overwhelming and unrealistic to think that the brain could take in all the information it needs regarding the various aspects of the world surrounding the child through a conscious process. The volume of information needed would be vast and the need to make connections through understanding would be impossible. So, it is important to remember that at birth, a child knows and understands nothing about this earth; neither the people and animals who share it, nor the objects that exist within it. All is new, all is unknown! Instead, nature provides a means of recording tremendous amounts of information without overwhelming the system.

It would also be impossible for a young child's mind to discern what is important and what is peripheral in any set of stimuli. The mental maturity to make this decision is not yet present in the new brain. It is nature's gift that the mind can take in all stimuli.

THE MONTESSORI APPROACH PREPARES THE BRAIN

With an empirical understanding of how the brain absorbs information and grows, Dr. Montessori developed an educational program for children that stimulates brain growth. Today, Montessori teachers learn the principle of "indirect preparation," which means there are a variety of activities and experiences in Montessori education that allow the child to arrive at a moment of readiness for the development of later skills and capacities, especially those associated with the work of the pre-frontal cortex.

Lise Eliot, Ph.D., a neuroscientist and a leading authority on early child development, has written extensively about the growth of perception, personality, language and intelligence. In her book, *What's Going on In There? How the Brain and Mind Develop in the First Five Years of Life,* Dr. Eliot discusses the impact language development has on later mental skills and abilities. "Learning to talk is probably the greatest intellectual leap of an individual's life," observes Dr. Eliot. "It opens up a new universe of questions, reasoning, social communication and opinions...that punch all other types of learning into warp speed and make a child finally seem like a full-fledged person."[13]

For those of us who are Montessori teachers, we don't always reap the benefits of the preparatory work we have offered to a child's educational experience. Instead, we have to trust that the fertile field has been sowed and the child will go about the remaining aspects of development, building on a solid foundation.

Montessori education impacts a child during the most critical periods of his development. We are supporting and nurturing children through the richness of the Montessori environment in ways that go so far beyond what they might experience randomly or spontaneously in the world.

For example, through the Children's House exercises offered in Montessori's Practical Life, children (ages three to six) build functional, everyday skills—pouring, baking, dusting, scrubbing, cutting vegetables and fruits, or arranging flowers into a beautiful bouquet. Through the sensorial materials in the Montessori classroom, the child meets all the keys to the exploration of the physical world. A child in a Montessori environment also builds his powers of intelligence, such as discernment of similarities and differences, memory, capacity for abstraction and categorization, a sense of mental order, and strategies for making order.

In language, a Montessori child learns the tools for clear communication and begins to build the skills needed for reading and writing. In mathematics, a child discovers the wonderful world of numbers—quantities that can be built and manipulated physically as a means to counting, but also to carrying out the four mathematical operations. Dr. Montessori developed the golden beads, which represent the hierarchies of the decimal system from the units to the thousands or the later representation of these hierarchies with the colored stamps—two approaches that engage a child's tactile and visual senses as a way to understand and begin counting. A Montessori child can easily count to one thousand using the colored bead chains and his knowledge of the sequence from one to one hundred as it is repeated.

In addition, a Montessori environment uses an experiential approach to expose a child to beautiful art and music, as well as the mysteries of science and geography. For example, in a Montessori classroom children are exposed to art by a variety of well-known artists. A child may look at an art print of work by Monet or Renoir, and discuss what she sees with the teacher. These art prints are a natural part of the prepared Montessori environment that provide opportunities for children to develop a sense of aesthetics.

Montessori children explore geography by observing how a simple compass needle swings to indicate the four directions of the earth. They quickly learn which is the north wall of the classroom so they can align the top of their puzzle maps of the world and each continent with the northern direction.

Even when children celebrate their birthdays in a Montessori classroom, the process involves several aspects of learning. Many Montessori teachers use a ritual to mark a child's birthday. Often, this ritual involves a lit candle, which represents the sun. The children gather in a circle and the birthday child walks slowly around the outside of the circle while carrying a small globe of the earth. This represents the orbit of the earth around the sun, each complete circle the equivalent of one "year" of life. In addition, parents are invited to write a little "story" of landmarks for each year of the child's life, which the teacher (or parent) reads as the child walks one circle for each year of his or her life. There is science, history, and poetic beauty embedded in this simple ritual celebration. In addition, the birthday child senses the passage of time in his or her life, and each child's importance as a part of the universe. Often, parents find this birthday ritual special and memorable.

SERVE THE CHILD WELL

Today's technology allows researchers to study the brain at work and to identify the manifestations of chemical and electrical energy coursing through different regions of the brain. This ever-evolving understanding of the brain stimulates us to think more fully and more responsibly about children and Montessori education.

The new scientific findings about the brain reinforce the Montessori belief to serve the child well, provide a rich environment for a child's developmental needs, and avoid wasting time and energy on activities that just fill the child's time. This is the ultimate gift to the child!

CHAPTER FIVE
Sensitive Periods Build Intelligence

Scholars of early childhood development have recognized for about 150 years that there are prime times for learning. Whether these times are called prime times, critical periods, windows of opportunity, or sensitive periods, they all refer to the same thing. Dr. Montessori called these times "sensitive periods" and developed her educational program around a child's sensitive periods within each plane. (I discussed Dr. Montessori's Four Planes of development in Chapter Three.)

A child's absorbent mind working in tandem with the sensitive periods is crucial for building knowledge. While a child's mind acts like a sponge taking in all the perceived data, it is the sensitive periods within each plane that give focus to this energy. Dr. Montessori recognized the importance of building upon each sensitive period within the First Plane in order to maximize on a child's educational development.

During the First Plane of development, nature magnifies several of the human tendencies for a pre-determined purpose. While the tendencies for communication, movement, and order exist throughout life, they have a specific function in early learning. These specific functions are represented by the sensitive periods for language, movement, and order.

It is not sufficient for the brain to simply take in information and to record it as separate and unrelated bytes of data. There has to be a means for sorting and linking similar experiences and related data, resulting in the creation of intelligence. There are prime times for optimal development, periods during which the brain is particularly efficient at specific types of learning. These periods are described as "critical periods," or "plastic periods," or in Montessori terms, "sensitive periods."

This concept is built on the premise that development depends on the exposure of the brain to many kinds of stimulation according to a predictable timetable. During developmental "primetimes," neurons can create synapses easily and efficiently. At these times, the senses are attuned to the specific aspects of the environment needed to satisfy the needs of the brain. For example, at four months of age, a child is getting ready to babble but needs to figure out how the mouth creates sounds. During this time period, the baby intently studies the lips and mouth of any person who is speaking. It is this fine-tuned attention that allows the baby's brain to gather all the information she needs about how these muscles function to create vocalizations. When enough information has been gathered, your baby begins to practice "talking" and the babbling begins.

The psyche, in effect, creates its own intrinsic motivation by responding to stimuli present within the immediate environment. Without the presence of another person speaking to the baby or speaking with others around the baby, she would not be able to observe and record this critical information. This is a great example of the importance of the human aspects of the environment and our complex social interactions that require the brain to expand.

Cognitive neuroscientist and psychologist, Merlin Donald, Ph.D., proposes that there is an "inextricable relationship between biology and culture." In other words, a young child cannot learn to speak without the influences of other human beings speaking around him. Dr. Donald offers insight into just how important this human aspect of the environment is for the creation of a spoken language. In his widely known book, *Origins of the Modern Mind: Three Stages in the Evolution of Culture and Cognition,* Dr. Donald writes, "Language is a very exotic adaptation indeed; there is no precedent for it in other species. And language is a social skill, dependent on the availability of a linguistic milieu for its development in the individual."[1]

SENSITIVE PERIODS IN THE FIRST PLANE

The impact of intrinsic motivations to grow and learn is observable throughout the growing years of a child. Children learn spontaneously and effortlessly, gathering from their environment those elements that provide the building blocks of intelligence. At different times and in various ways, a child is drawn to different aspects of the world with intense interest and concentration as noted in the example above.

The developing brain during the First Plane produces many times more neurons and synapses than it will ever need from this intense attraction. Imagine a growing network of connections all intertwined in a massive ball. How could such a system function efficiently or effectively?

Fortunately, nature solved this problem by evolving a more economical system. Around age three, a child's brain development then becomes a process of pruning: the brain selectively eliminates excess synapses. As a child grows, an overabundance of connections gives way to a complex, powerful system of neural pathways. Rich and varied stimulation is important, but does not need to be voluminous. What many adults do not understand is the power of a child's absorbent mind to glean every nuance of information out of every possible experience. What adults might perceive as a need for the volume in exposure, the child replaces with quality of perception.

As a child grows, her brain must create all the neurological networks from which come memory, critical thinking (thought and decision making), verbal problem solving, extensive vocabulary, linguistic conventions (including rules of phonology or speech sounds, and grammar), an elaborate verbal semantic memory, spatial and constructive skills, and a mental schematic for organizing all the classifications and categorizations that exist within the mind. The young child's brain is brilliant in its ability to develop and grow!

FROM SENSORY TO ABSTRACT

For the moment, let's focus on the creation of abstractions from a sensory experience. For example, a young child creates an abstraction for an animal, such as a cat, by first perceiving a physical cat by using her senses. The child sees the cat, touches the cat, hears the cat's meow, smells the cat, maybe even tastes the cat's fur! The child's brain cells store all of this sensory data.

As the child repeats this experience with a cat, the initial information becomes refined and strengthened. In time, the child's brain begins to perceive the patterns of familiarity with the information coming in. The brain cells define the recording of information relative to "catness" as the child's experiences with cats continue to be stimulated and strengthened.[2]

For starters, the child must first make the most elemental distinctions between what is a "cat" and what is a "dog" or any other animal she may encounter in her first years. This process of making distinctions is a natural part of the refinement of the brain's neural networks and the creation of a concept.

While the brain is connecting all the neural networks that define what a cat is, it is also sorting out what is not a cat. The discrimination that makes a cat distinct from a chair is the same as the power that distinguishes a cat from a dog or a guinea pig. Over time, and with repeated exposure to the stimuli, a child's brain creates a concept upon which she recognizes something familiar. While the concept is created during the unconscious period of learning, the conscious mind has to be able to retrieve this information so it can be used.

With ongoing exposure to cats and other animals, a child gathers new information regarding common activities or functions relative to each animal. For example, maybe the family cat will run away and hide when he sees the child or maybe the cat will purr when the child strokes the cat's soft fur. Each personal interaction adds new information. All of this knowledge is linked in the brain. Each component serves to record one aspect of the whole.

The young child's brain also has to sort out what is specific to all cats and what is not. For example, not all cats are the same color. The child may first interact with a black and white cat, creating the assumption that all cats are black and white. Then the child visits Grandma and discovers an orange tabby cat. Now, the child's brain has to assimilate this new information into the whole of what a cat looks like. Sorting and categorizing what is "catness" gets more complex when the child visits the zoo and sees a large wild cat with stripes. This forces further assimilation as the neural networks become more refined.

What does the child use to link and call forth all of this information? One last piece must be added to the network—the language!

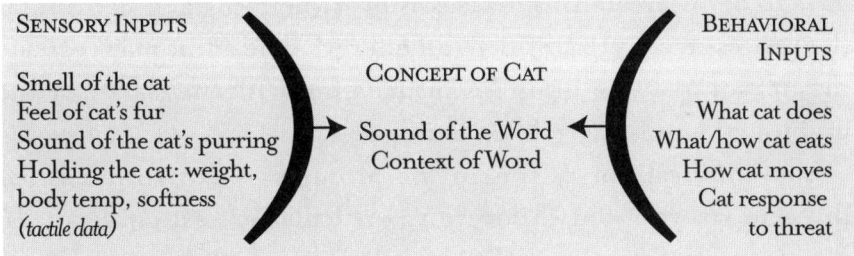

SENSORY INPUTS	CONCEPT OF CAT	BEHAVIORAL INPUTS
Smell of the cat Feel of cat's fur Sound of the cat's purring Holding the cat: weight, body temp, softness *(tactile data)*	Sound of the Word Context of Word	What cat does What/how cat eats How cat moves Cat response to threat

For example, the name "cat" exists as the summation of all the components of this particular animal. The name serves the generic function of linking all the associated pieces and making them accessible to the conscious mind.

The child goes one step further and builds a schematic of familiarity such that she can retrieve images from her brain without the object being immediate or present. For instance, a child's brain will picture a cat without the cat being in the room. So, when a parent asks, "Where's the cat?" The child will look around for a specific object—a cat! Or the child sees a picture of a cat in a book and recognizes this image as representing a cat. This level of knowing is based on the creation of abstractions (the extracted essence of the information taken in.) It is the abstractions that allow the child to create the building blocks of thought.

Imagine having to create all this overabundance of knowledge through conscious effort and energy. This is what babies and young children do every day. Children are brilliant in their ability to gather information and sort this information into complex building blocks. The child's mind has to carry out the task of creating the concept and abstraction from experience alone and does this without any visible expense of energy or effort!

Adults might come close to this experience when they learn the vocabulary of a new language, but even then, they already have the basic concept in their mind upon which to attach the new language. A better analogy might be the adult who has experienced brain damage and has destroyed neural networks that have to be re-created. This task is overwhelming and painful, as the process takes great effort and energy. The adult may recreate the networks in the brain but usually not with the clarity or the usability that was there from childhood.

The implications of this in the Montessori environment for three-to six-year-old children in particular are astounding. In Montessori's Children's House, all the sensorial refining and sensory discrimination in the Sensorial Area of the classroom support this development, as do all the exercises focused on refinement and coordination of movement in Practical Life. The child outside of the Montessori prepared environment is carrying out the same developmental processes. This is important to acknowledge. However, this experience is random and may not be systematic or organized in any manner for clarity.

The organization of the early sensorial materials in the Montessori classroom allows children to explore the basic elements (the qualities) of the physical world. The progression of the activities leads to a systematic and in-depth experience. The clarity of the experience allows for the formation of a clean, but also a keenly refined abstraction.

For example, a child in a Montessori environment can take the basic characteristics of a cat and sort the information to make finer more detailed distinctions. In general, cats are soft, but there are different degrees of softness or roughness. The Montessori fabric boxes allow a child to explore degrees of softness as reflected in common fabrics. One box of fabrics represents textures created from natural fibers, all of which allow for fairly discernible differences. Yet, a later box of fabrics is all different weaves of cotton. The child builds a quite refined and precise skill in being able to tell the difference while blindfolded. This is an activity that many adults have great difficulty carrying out.

Similar Montessori sensorial materials allow a child to explore other characteristics, such as weight, shape or color. The child can then apply this generic information to her experience with a cat. The Montessori sensorial materials will allow a child to separate each of these physical qualities as an entity itself. The Montessori baric tablets are sensorial materials that include sets of wooden tablets that vary in weight. Baric tablets allow a child to explore differences in weight. In addition, a typical Montessori geometry cabinet is full of different shapes and boxes of color tablets for children to explore color.

In each of these Montessori materials, all the other physical qualities are the same so the child perceives this additional information but does not use this information for carrying out sorting, matching or grading activities. As the child progresses through the materials, she is naturally led to make finer and finer distinctions.

To this construct, we add the specific vocabulary that describes various aspects of cats. Using the cat example, when a child learns about cats in a Montessori Children's House, she will learn correct names for different species of cats. The child also learns the correct names for the physical qualities of cats. For instance, instead of just understanding there are many types of cats, children in the Montessori environment learn specifics, such as classifications for wild cats, which includes tigers, cougars, jaguars, leopards and lions, among others. A child also learns the external body parts of the cat, such as whiskers, paws, claws, haunches, shorthaired, or longhaired.

Now, the child has the key to long-term memory as well as the developed powers of abstraction upon which the creative imagination is based. For example, think of the importance of vocabulary enrichment, especially beyond nouns, for future writing and speaking skills.

Intelligence Under Construction

In Montessori, the orientation to exactness and precision are the preparations of a mathematical mind for arithmetic. Again, there is a definitive connection to both Practical Life and the Sensorial exercises in the Montessori environment. Children working with the Practical Life activities refine their motor cortex and gradually bring the movements of their hands under the command of their minds. In Montessori, carrying out longer works with a prescribed and logical sequence supports the work of the Sensitive Period for Order. In turn, this will lead to the creation of a mind capable of orderly thought processes.

The Montessori activities with the sensorial materials allow a child's mind to develop the powers of refined discrimination. In essence, the brain has been trained to interpret and respond to very minute degrees of difference in stimuli. For example, in time a child learns to recognize the difference between a Burmese cat and a Siamese cat or can note the textural difference between a piece of linen and a piece of cotton fabric. The motivational force of the sensitive periods is nature's way of making sure that a child takes in the specific kinds of information needed to create distinctly human characteristics. This is intelligence under construction.

CHAPTER SIX

Conquering Everest

Over several decades of working with children, Dr. Montessori observed a fundamental truth about how babies develop. She observed:

> Man brings no abilities with him into the world, yet his gifts are unsurpassed in the learning of movements...All children are alike at birth, they unfold in the same way and according to the same laws.[1]

This observation still holds true in the twenty-first century, confirmed by recent neuroscientific findings. Dr. Montessori summarized her observations in a chart in her book, *The Absorbent Mind,* which reflects the typical timeline for the development of both equilibrium (the development of locomotion) and the development of the hand. This chart is a simplified version of Dr. Montessori's chart.

Dr. Montessori recognized early on that the same patterns of motor development she witnessed in Italy and throughout Europe, were also evidenced in India, Sri Lanka and other Asian cultures she visited. The universality of these observations indicated that all children, regardless of country or culture or race, learn to move the muscles of their bodies in similar patterns. Movement allows a child to move his or her body from one place to another and to explore the environment. Indeed, the hand becomes the tool of the mind once a child can walk, freeing his or her hands for discovery. Almost any current parenting book will provide a similar chart that gives typical ages for the mastery of specific kinds of movement.

0	6mos.	12.mos	18mos.	24mos.	30mos.
EQUILIBRIUM					
Enormous brain development	Rapid Cerebellum development Equilibrium acquired in 4 stages		Cycles of activity Maximum effort	Coordinated/ Applied movement	
HAND					
First – to be alive	Development of grasping	Prehension becomes intentional (Choice)	Strength	Co-ordination by means of experience	

BABY'S DEVELOPMENT OF EQUILIBRIUM

A newborn has limited movement because of limited control over most muscles and nerves. The human baby is certainly at a disadvantage when compared to most newborns in the animal world. A child comes into this world with his biological system for movement still immature and under construction. During the first six months of life, a human is quite immobile.

Dr. Montessori refers to the creation of the tools for locomotion as the "development of equilibrium." Two factors contribute to equilibrium—maturation of the neural system, and physical activity to refine these tools.

As noted in a previous chapter, a newborn child is limited by the absence of myelin sheathing around the cortex of the vertebral system. The myelin sheathing is the protective coating that insulates each cell of the nervous system. This protective coating assures that the electrical and chemical energy transmitted back and forth through these cells follows its intended pathway. Myelin sheathing is similar to the rubber coating on an electrical cord. The myelin sheathing matures from the base of the spine at the back of the neck, downwards, accounting for the pattern of muscular control from the head out to the legs and hands.

The growth of the myelin sheathing through the body from the base of the spine downward and from the same point forward into the brain itself is called the process of myelinization. A good example is that of a baby who struggles with even the simplest task of lifting his head up before the myelin sheathing is completely in place, at least past the neck muscles. Rapid growth of the brain's cerebellum from six months until about fifteen months of age allows for the development of the mechanics of equilibrium.

With the companion process of myelinization, the nerves of the spinal column are protected and stimulated. The nerves in the muscles respond to sensory stimulation and send these messages to the brain. The brain sends messages out through different nerves in response to this stimuli and the baby moves specific muscles in response. The whole process of sending messages from the nerve cells in the muscles to the brain, and back from the brain to the muscles, takes a matter of nanoseconds. Slowly, the baby begins to gain control of the muscles in his neck and shoulders and can hold up his head and see more of the surrounding world.

Gradually, the myelin works its way down the spinal column and the baby gains control of his extremities—the arms and legs— and gradually, control of the muscles in the spine and abdomen related to equilibrium. This leads progressively to the baby rolling over, then sitting up unassisted, followed with creeping, crawling, cruising, and finally, upright walking. In a few short months, after the completion of the process of myelinization, a baby can get almost anywhere without assistance. These modes of locomotion slowly free a child from dependence on another person to move them from one place to another. With locomotion, a child can explore more of the world, no longer limited to the proximity of experience in one place.

THE BEAUTY OF LOCOMOTION

Locomotion serves as a powerful motivation for the human psyche. As adults, we have lost an awareness of life in different zones of space around us. We see what is right in front of our eyes as we stand or sit. I often challenge my students who are studying to be Montessori teachers to put themselves in the place of the developing child. I ask them to lay flat on the floor, on their backs, and see what is available for sensory stimulation. Then I have them turn over on their stomach and lift up their head and shoulders. Then they sit up, then crawl along the floor, and eventually stand in one spot. Finally, I have the students walk from one spot toward whatever interests them.

At the end of this exercise, the students are always amazed at how limited the motives for stimulation are when movement is limited. This exercise heightens adult awareness of how highly motivated a baby is to slowly bring more of the world into her experience just by getting up off the floor and moving from one spot to another.

Many of my students chuckle about how their own children enjoyed observing them carry out the experiment at home. Parents often offer stimuli at *their* eye level and forget that this is not the field of vision for the immobile child. We adults also forget that a child needs to be free from confinement if she is going to practice movement and become stimulated by the experience.

As adults, we have forgotten that coordinated movement takes lots of repetition and practice, and that children must carry out this practice for themselves without our help. For a young child, movement for the sake of movement is sufficient for the activity. The delicate interplay between the brain as central command, the nerve cables that carry the messages back and forth, and the muscles as the executors of the movement, requires great practice.

Lise Eliot, Ph.D., a leading authority in early child development, describes the complexity required to master movement:

> There also needs to be coordination between the cortispinal axons, which trigger the motor neurons which in turn send the message to the peripheral nerves in a particular muscle fiber. The electrical excitation causes the muscle to contract or relax.... As the muscle

responds to the changes in tension and length, the proprioceptors (sensory neurons) send the message back to the brain that the muscle is responding. The proprioceptors allow the human to fine-tune the muscular response. A movement in one set of muscles also involves a reciprocal response from the matching set of muscles...the brain relies on the cerebellum to keep all this information coordinated.[2]

I believe that many adults may have gone overboard in their attempts to secure and make their children safe. In their desire to be as safe as possible, they have cut off avenues for exploration and learning. Parents have closed off the carpeted stairs, corralled children in a playpen so they won't get in the way, and they have strapped children into a conveyance so they don't get into trouble. Even worse, adults put children in situations where they expect the little ones to be still, as if this was a child's natural state of being. It's not! Children's neurological circuitry demands movement—that's how they learn.

B. Perkins Family Collection

Cross crawling through the water.

Coordination of Movement

While the basic modes of locomotion are generally developed some time between nine and fifteen months of age, the coordination of movement takes a much longer period of practice. During the toddler years, a child adds climbing, running, pushing, and pulling to the repertoire of learned skills.

Moving across the room and keeping all the muscles headed in the same direction takes practice. Once a child has mastered basic movement, then she has to learn how to move while carrying objects. Carrying a bucket of water or a tray with something on it, or a watering can filled with water become great challenges for a young child. Rolling up a rug, walking around the rug, and walking without bumping into anyone or anything also take lots of practice! In order to practice all these new skills, parents and supervising adults have to learn patience as they let their children move and explore.

Climbing to New Heights

Certainly, as adults we take these skills for granted and somehow believe that a child should be able to do them perfectly after only one attempt. Adults also don't appreciate the diligence of a child practicing certain movements until he attains a certain level of satisfaction. Even more so, adults usually don't notice the expression of accomplishment on the face of the child once he's mastered an important physical task!

A number of years ago, I was eating breakfast in a small bistro in New York City and had the opportunity to watch a young child about eighteen months old climb what I saw as her Mt. Everest. Okay, the child's Mt. Everest was the bench her mother and older sister were sitting on. While they were engaged in animated conversation, the toddler eyed the bench, and obviously felt the challenge. She quickly flung her sippy cup aside, intrigued by the bench. She pulled herself up to the bench and struggled mightily to find a way to get one knee over the edge of the bench. Given her bulky diaper and the height of the bench this was no mere task, but the toddler persisted until she found a technique that allowed her knee to anchor over the top. That was only the first challenge.

Next, she had to figure out how to hoist her body weight (and that of the diaper!) over the edge. Observing the struggle, I was so tempted to just give a hand to help, but that would probably have resulted in tears on the part of the child. I resisted! I can only guess at the amount of strength and coordination it took for the little girl, but again, with significant trial and error, she figured out how to get her knee far enough over the edge to make it work as a lever. Finally, she succeeded!

The toddler got up onto the bench, turned herself around to sit like her mother and big sister, and beamed with delight at her accomplishment. Mother and Sister noticed her presence, took it all for granted, quietly smiled, and kept on conversing. One would think that having succeeded, the little girl would stay put. This assumption only fits when we think of the movement as a goal to accomplish and check off the list of goals for the moment. Not so for the young child. The little girl immediately figured out how to turn back around on the bench, slide her legs over the edge and let gravity put her back on the ground. Then she proceeded to scale the "mountain" again and again. No one noticed, no one stopped her activity, and no one told the child what a good job she was doing! She didn't need recognition. She was carrying out the activity for the sole purpose of meeting the challenge.

Each repetition became more efficient as the toddler learned from her successes and failures. Observing all of this reminded me of the great resilience of children and the need for practice, even practice that would seem meaningless to the adults.

HANDS ARE FOR LEARNING

As children master modes of locomotion, their hands gradually become the instruments of the mind. A child's ability to grasp objects develops parallel to the development of locomotion as the child becomes an active explorer of the environment. In his book, *The Hand: How Its Use Shapes the Brain, Language, and Human Culture,* neuroscientist Frank R. Wilson, Ph.D., writes: "There is no point lifting the baby's little bottom off the ground until the brain is prepared to confront the explosion of visual-spatial information that will result."[3] Dr. Wilson describes this as the "brain teaching itself to synthesize visual and tactile perceptions by making the hand and the eye learn to work together."[4]

Before the body is ready to move, the eye needs to learn to fixate on an object. It is only then, notes Dr. Wilson, that the "reaching arm has wide latitude in the combination of joint angles and contraction-relaxation patterns of trunk and upper extremity muscles that can be assumed in order to bring the hand in contact with the physical target."[5]

Parents might witness this in their baby's development when they hang a mobile above their infant's crib. At first, it seems that the infant doesn't even see the mobile because there is no attempt to reach out toward it. Within a short period of time, the infant does reach out, almost by accident, reaching toward this "new" object. The first attempts to make the mobile move are random thrusts of the arm, but as the parents watch, they see that the thrusts of the arm become more directed. It is almost as if the baby's eyes see, and the brain analyzes the angle between the body and the mobile, the angle between the arm and the mobile, and the amount of force needed to hit the mobile. Very quickly, the infant becomes successful in hitting the mobile time after time.

When we add in the factor of the eyes spotting just when the mobile has quit swinging from the baby's last hit making the mobile available to be hit again, we begin to see the complexity of the task. Another experience along these lines relates to a baby's use of his legs and how his eyes sense where his legs are in space. Often, a parent will hold her baby and attempt to stand the baby on the parent's thighs only to have the baby totally collapse his legs. It is as if the baby doesn't yet know that there is a stable surface below his legs. Again, it doesn't take long for the infant to feel secure, stiffening the legs and standing royally on Dad or Mom's lap.

We don't often stop to think of the simple movements of the legs and hands in such a complex way. A child must learn to reach out and to grasp an object with the whole hand first, then later with just the fingers. A child must learn not only which fingers to use, but also how tightly to hold them and how to release the grip. Any mother who has experienced the "death grip" her baby has on her glasses or her earring, knows what I am saying. A small child grips with a tightness that is the full extent of his power. Letting go seems to be a later development!

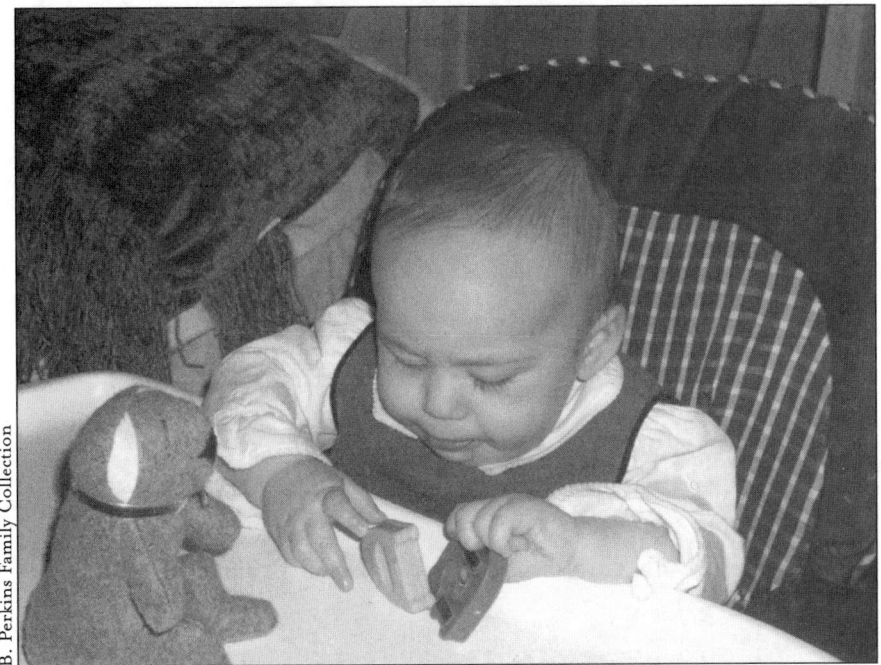

Full-fisted grasping happens around six months.

SENSITIVE PERIOD FOR MOVEMENT

The nature of the human hand makes the significance of the free hand even more important. The hand is much more than just an instrument freed from the needs of locomotion and now available to explore the world. The hand becomes the instrument of the mind! The human is the only species designed exclusively to use the thumb and fingers as we do (the opposable thumb) and the human is the only species that uses the hands independent of the feet.

From the earliest cultural societies, the human has sought to use the hands to express herself and to shape the world for personal use. The evidence of these efforts is reflected in the artifacts left behind—the first tools, paintings in caves, elaborate tombs, and writings. We see that the skill of the human's hands is bound up with the development of the mind. Acknowledging the importance of the hand, Dr. Montessori wrote:

> We may say that man's hand has followed his intel-
> lect, his spiritual life and his emotions, and the marks
> it has left behind betray his presence. But even without
> this psychological view of things, we can see that all the
> changes in man's environment are brought about by his
> hands. Really, it seems as if the whole business of intel-
> ligence is to guide their work. It is thanks to the hand,
> the companion of the mind, that civilization has arisen.[6]

In essence, the tools of movement—the hands and feet—are being prepared simultaneously, but independently. While a child practices the coordination of gross motor movement in order to move the body through space, the hand is practicing the art of gripping or grasping.

Dr. Wilson defines grip as "the ability to flex the finger joints and hold them in that position against the pull of the full weight of the body."[7] A toddler practices a great variety of fine motor movements since the hand will put the child into contact with the physical elements of the natural world. The hand that begins to grasp with a death grip at about six months of age becomes a refined instrument around four-and-a-half years old. (This is not to be confused with the reflexive grasp that is present a few weeks after birth, which disappears until it is replaced by this intentional grasp.)

The hand masters all the various types of grips: precision grips such as the pincer grip and the pencil grip; power grips such as the squeeze grip and the grasping grip; and hook grips such as the suitcase grip. Children seek opportunities to apply these movements to the simple activities of dressing, eating, and caring for objects in their surrounding world. Eventually, a child refines the hand as the instrument capable of handwriting and manipulating small objects.

The sensitive period for movement is not concluded once a child is mobile and the hands are free. This is insufficient for the needs of the human psyche. The child spends considerable energy over the next two to three years mastering the mechanisms related to movement. It is during this extended period of time that a child's vertebral column strengthens and the muscles of the body coordinate with intended movements.

Montessori Magnet School, Hartford, CT

Polishing a metal spoon is a fine motor movement.

The harmonious functioning of the brain, the nerve cells, and the muscles must be created. The integration of the personality, as Dr. Montessori called it, occurs through the child's active practice and later application of movement.

It might seem a straightforward matter of strengthening the muscles, however, this process goes far beyond mere strengthening. It goes to the heart of coordination. A child practices movements within a meaningful context, a purposeful activity, and the muscles become more adept at responding accurately and automatically to the brain's messages. An activity becomes purposeful when it encompasses an activity that can be repeated over and over.

In addition, the activity must be connected with something that a child observes other humans doing as a natural part of life. The connection here is powerful. A child discovers that the activities she has practiced and refined now have logical applications within the natural environment. Prior to this logical connection, children intuit all the aspects of human activity. A child is drawn naturally to practice the movements that are observed as a part of everyday life. Ultimately, a child's strongest motivation comes from the desire to become like the other humans she observes. She will apply movements in the same manner and in the same context that she has observed in adults.

PARENTS SUPPORTING INDEPENDENT MOVEMENT

For parents, the implications are that we must let our children be involved in the everyday tasks of life, whether washing vegetables for dinner, hanging up their own clothing, or setting the table. Children have a strong desire to contribute, even though they are not as efficient or as skilled in their movements as older children or adults.

It is easy for an adult to convey messages of incompetence to a child who is doing the best he can and wants to participate. Adults are tempted to do things for children in order to save time and aggravation, but this does not ultimately help the child. In recent years, I have been working in China training Montessori teachers. In China, parents and grandparents take great pride in doting on their children or grandchildren. Unfortunately, this often results in the parents physically carrying their children even at age two or three when children are fully capable of walking. I see parents feeding children who are capable of feeding themselves. I watched one four-year-old boy eat a slice of watermelon and spit the seeds into his father's hand instead of spitting the seeds into the dish himself or removing the seeds from his mouth with his own fingers.

Regarding parents over helping their children with daily tasks, Dr. Montessori wrote:

> We [adults] believe that children are like puppets. We wash them and feed them as if they were dolls. We never stop to think that a child who does not act does not know how to act, but he should act, and nature has given him all the means for learning how to act.... Such service is dangerous as well as easy. It closes outlets, places obstacles in the way of a life which is unfolding, and besides these immediate consequences it has others which are more serious for the future"[8]

MOVEMENT AND INDEPENDENCE

There is one more reality to consider about the mastery of equilibrium in a young child. All through the period during which a child masters locomotion, his body is designed like a top-heavy vase. The proportions between the trunk of the body and head outweigh and out distance the space from the hips to the heels. There will need to be two subsequent periods of drastic growth before a child's body develops into balanced (50/50) proportioning. During both of these transitional periods, a child will be challenged by the nature of equilibrium and will have to reconfigure coordination as his body grows.

There is a secondary value to a child's practice of movement. Neuroscientists have determined that a child's physical movement stimulates a great number of neurological systems— many more than are needed to carry out the movement itself. While it would seem that this is a counterproductive waste of brain cells, the brain is actually building networks for later reference. The supplemental motor area and the pre-motor cortex in the brain are used primarily for higher-level activities related to planning and executing more complex sequences of movement. A child will not fully utilize some of these neurological networks until he is an adolescent. When children reach adolescence, there is a sense of independence that comes with movement, as the world is now theirs for the taking.

Again, it would be simple to see movement simply as the ability to get from one location to another and to explore with the hands in order to feed the mind. However, the impact on the neurological development within the brain is even more astounding.

Dr. Wilson observes: "It is in the child's earliest experiences in practical physics—watching, locating with both hand and eye, and then intercepting moving objects—that the nervous system builds its own unique library of solutions to the computational problems presented by coordinated movement."[9]

A child needs the opportunity to practice movements in order for the movements to become fully integrated into his psyche. Dr. Eliot writes, "The more a particular pathway is activated during consistent, purposeful action, the likelier it is to be stabilized…. What practice does is to find, by trial and error, the few most efficient patterns and to strengthen and stabilize them."[10]

Dr. Montessori summarizes the whole of motor development this way: "So the logic of the natural development is seen: First the child prepares his instruments, hands and feet. Then he gets strength by exercise, and next he looks at what other people are doing and sets to work in imitation, fitting himself for life and freedom."[11]

CHAPTER SEVEN
Talk, Talk, Talk

Dr. Montessori identified the mastering of language as one of the great observable conquests in the life of a young child. The sensitive period for language—from birth to six years—demonstrates how a child takes information from the surrounding world and uses it to create the specific human capacity for spoken language. During the sensitive period for language, a child's brain can take in different types of information at various points that lead to understanding and speaking a specific language or languages.

Early childhood development expert, Lise Eliot, Ph.D., explains in her book, *What's Going on in There?*, why mastering language is so powerful for children:

> Learning to talk is probably the greatest intellectual leap of an individual's life. It opens up a new universe of questions, reasoning, social communication and opinions...that punch all other types of learning into warp speed and make a child finally seem like a full-fledged person.[1]

In essence, a young child's language development is a microcosm of the whole of language development throughout the history of humankind. The human evolution of language began when early humans created vocalizations that evolved into words with understood meanings. Later, humans took these words—the vocabulary— and plugged them into a structure called the syntax. The formation of sentences and phrases from words allowed humans to communicate thoughts and ideas.

This evolution in language took many thousands of years to develop and to this day is still evolving in all languages worldwide. In light of the long history of language development, it is quite amazing when you consider that a young child unfolds this whole process in the same evolutionary order within the first six years of his or her life!

THE ROLE OF THE CEREBELLUM

At the base of the human brain is an area called the cerebellum, which means "little brain" in Latin. Basically, this part of the brain coordinates complex voluntary movements, posture, and balance. The maturation of a human's cerebellum is critical to language development along with motor functioning, as is the myelinization of the neural cells in the brain. (Myelinization is discussed in Chapter Four.)

Motor functioning is directly related to the maturation of nerve cells in the spinal column and out to the extremities of the body. Often, what gets lost in the discussion of motor functioning is the fact that the myelinization process is also maturing neural cells in the brain.

Language development has a physiological aspect in the coordination of the muscles around the mouth, the tongue, and the lips, as well as the muscles in the larynx, which includes the "voice box." However, the maturation of the cells in the brain's language center becomes a dominant focus in a child's language development. Crucial evidence supporting the assumption that language is distinctly a mental construct is the fact that it is physically localized in the left hemisphere of the brain for about 97% of people. We generally think of the left hemisphere of the brain as the "thinking hemisphere." It is the left hemisphere of the

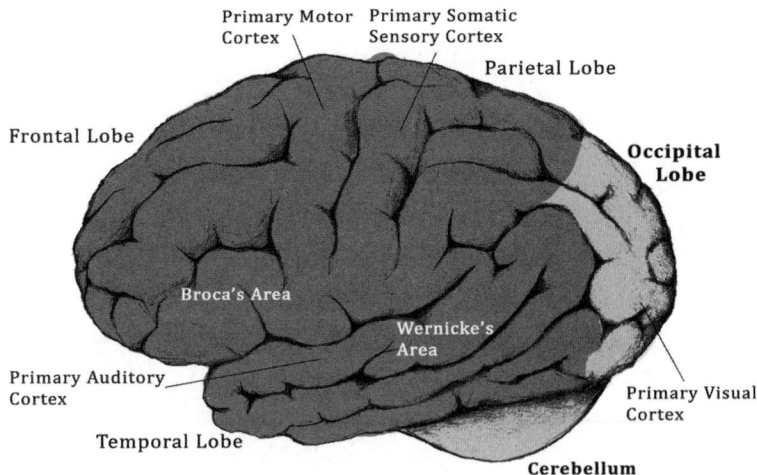

Labels on diagram:
Primary Motor Cortex
Primary Somatic Sensory Cortex
Parietal Lobe
Frontal Lobe
Occipital Lobe
Broca's Area
Wernicke's Area
Primary Auditory Cortex
Primary Visual Cortex
Temporal Lobe
Cerebellum

Brain diagram showing the cerebellum and the occipital lobe.

brain that is associated with symbolic representations. The left hemisphere allows us to think logically, use abstract images, and to reason. Because we think in words, the left side of the brain's connection to language is important. The emotional qualities of intonation and inflection are the only aspects associated with the right hemisphere of the brain.

There are two major areas of the brain that are responsible for language and they are significant for our discussion on language development in children. These parts of the brain are called "Broca's area," and "Wernicke's area," named after the two neuroscientists who identified these areas of the brain.

In the 1860s, Paul Broca, M.D., identified an area of the brain associated with the frontal lobe that is responsible for grammar and other mental skills such as planning, sequencing, and logic. In terms of child development, Dr. Broca's findings were important because the neural cells in this part of the brain are myelenized later in a child's First Plane of development, beginning around age five and continuing through adolescence. Thus, the associated skills identified with this area of the brain develop later.

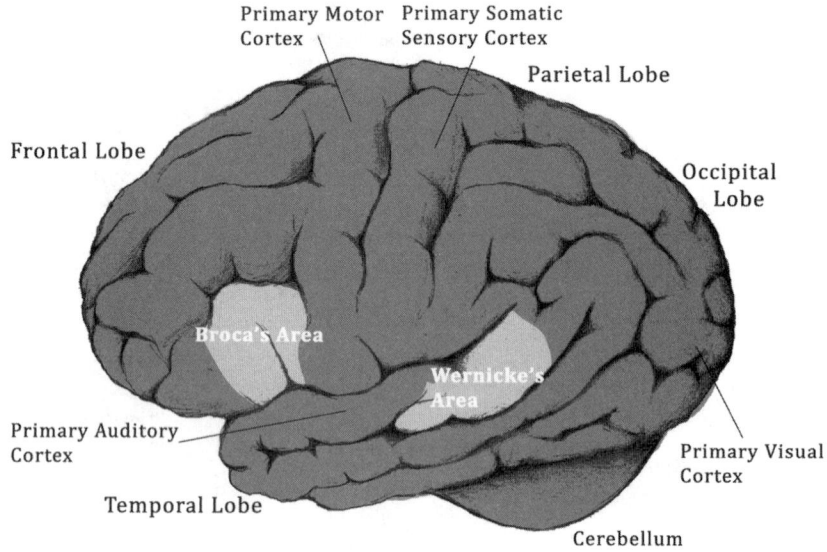

Brain diagram highlights the Broca area and the Wernicke area.

Carl Wernicke, M.D., studied the brain and rose to international fame in the 1870s after he wrote about aphasia, which is the loss of ability to speak. Dr. Wernicke identified a different area of the brain that also relates to language development. In Dr. Lise's book, *What's Going on in There?*, she notes, "Wernicke's area is located near the junction of three important senses—hearing, vision and touch—so it is a good place for the brain to store the associations between the sound of words and the physical entities—the persons, places and things—they represent."[2]

The Wernicke area of the brain, located nearer the cerebellum and the occipital lobe, is responsible for storing vocabulary. Since this part of the brain is closer to the brain stem, the neural cells are mylenized earlier in development and the capacity for vocabulary precedes the creation of the language structure.

If language development were merely a matter of brain maturation, a child would simply wait for this to occur as he grew older and then simply begin to speak. But this is not what happens. Language is a social skill designed to be used in a social context. Humans speak in order to communicate with other humans, to express ideas, or to share feelings. When a child's environment has limited human contact or interaction, this results in impaired language skills for the child.

Dr. Montessori understood and observed the fundamental need for human interaction in a child's language development. For years, she had witnessed children's language development in many different cultures, and she empirically understood the sensitive period for language development.

As a young doctor interested in the brain, Dr. Montessori also studied the case of Victor, the wild boy of Aveyron, a feral child who apparently lived the first twelve years of his life in a forest in France. In 1800, at about age twelve (his exact age was not known), Victor began living with humans. He had no spoken language and little capacity to learn a spoken language. Jean-Marc Itard, M.D., worked closely with Victor for years to develop language. Victor's inability to learn spoken language led to the first understanding of what modern child development specialists call language acquisition, which takes place in the early years of a child's life.

Today, the same language deficit is found in many orphaned children raised in severely depressed circumstances. Many of these children had limited language development in the early years—during the language sensitive period—and have had great difficulties learning the aspects of symbolic language, which build upon the foundation of a spoken language. Addressing this concern, Dr. Eliot writes:

> The brain's language network properly and permanently wires up only when it is exposed to the coherent combination of sound, meaning and grammar in any single human language. Just as the act of seeing completes the circuitry for visual perception, so do hearing and using language in early life help hone

every element in the large language network, from the circuits that analyze word sounds, to those that inter-pret their meaning and syntax, to those controlling their quick and precise vocal production."[3]

NEWBORNS AND LANGUAGE

At birth, a newborn arrives with a brain prepped and ready for language. The left hemisphere was already specialized for lan-guage by the end of the second trimester in the womb. At birth, the baby's brain is geared to hear and to discriminate the individ-ual phonemes or distinct sounds of the particular language the baby hears. A newborn will automatically turn her head toward the sound of a bell, but reacts both physically and emotionally with movements to the sound of her mother's voice. The baby hears all kinds of mechanical sounds and non-human sounds in the environment, but none of these evoke the same reaction as the sound of a human voice. No matter who the speaker is, the tone of voice, or the dialect, the baby is able to organize the individual phonemes into different categories. An infant needs to hear millions of words and phonemes during the first year to build a strong foundation.

At birth, a baby can already distinguish familiar voices from all other voices, especially that of her mother or other indi-viduals who were around when the baby was still in the womb. Hearing is one of the most acute senses at birth. Within a couple months, a child distinguishes vocal sounds from all the other random sounds in her world. In fact, by four months of age, a baby has already discerned who is producing the vocal sounds and she turns her attention toward the mouth of the person talking. At four months, a baby can hold up her own head, so she begins to watch the muscles around the speaker's mouth, the lips, and the position of the tongue. It is as if the baby's brain is imprinting the position of the speaker's muscles as sounds are created.

If this is true, people often ask, "Do children receive the same information if they are watching the mouth of a person speaking on the television?" The answer is No! In fact, babies don't even connect sounds from the television with the person on television as the source. This is a great reminder of how important it is for an infant to have real people around her who are speaking directly to her.

New parents might worry that they don't know what to say to an infant in a one-way conversation. Linguists reassure parents that this is not a problem. They encourage parents to talk to their baby about their activities as they are doing them. For instance, a parent might talk to the baby about changing the baby's diaper, giving the baby a bath, or make observations as they watch the cat or dog playing. Perhaps the parent can talk about how the baby might be feeling or what she is thinking. It is important to remember that the baby doesn't recognize individual words or their meanings, but the baby is simply connecting with the speaker and watching how the sounds are produced. So parents, it's okay to talk, talk, talk. Your baby will be listening and observing!

Around six months of age, a baby begins to exercise the muscles around the mouth and soon begins to babble. During the extended six to eight months of babbling, a child will randomly create and practice almost all the phonemes required by all spoken languages. Chinese babies make the "er" sound quite naturally. All babies make the rolling "r." This is the ultimate in random practice, but very quickly a baby begins to systematically eliminate those sounds not heard repeatedly in her spoken environment, therefore losing the ability to produce these unnecessary sounds. So, if a baby is in a multi-lingual household and hears phonemes from different languages repeatedly, she will remember them and eventually use them to spontaneously speak the various languages she is exposed to. A baby quits sounding the phonemes she doesn't hear in her native language so she can focus on practicing those phonemes that are needed.

Many adults know the challenges of learning a new language. For instance, the guttural sounds of German are difficult for someone who does not use those phonemes in his or her native language. For those who speak English, learning to speak a language with different tones such as German is a great challenge.

My college German teacher was quite impressed by my ability to pronounce words using the guttural German sound. For me, this was no surprise because my father's family spoke German all the time while I was growing up. Even though I cannot speak German, I practiced the sounds as a baby and retained this vocalizing ability because the German phonemes remained as a part of my natural environment.

Similarly, for those who speak Mandarin, it is difficult to pronounce English words using an "r" sound because it is not a phoneme common to Mandarin. I am learning to speak Mandarin and find many of the phonemes for Mandarin difficult. For example, the phoneme for "ci" sounds like "t" to my ear, yet when I pronounce it that way, no one understands, and my translator attempts to correct me. I can't tell you exactly what this sound is like because I can't hear it or say it correctly, but the sound is somewhere between a "t" and a "tz" in English.

Within the context of babbling, a baby begins to reflect a new understanding at about nine months. It is at this point that the babbling begins to carry intonation, which is the pattern or melody of pitch changes in a sentence. For example, a baby's babbling will begin to imitate sentences in a conversation. The baby still can't make words, but she is reflecting an understanding that words carry meaning and are used for person-to-person connection. This is a good example of a baby's intelligence that precedes her physical capacity to apply the knowledge.

At this stage, a babbling baby will carry on whole conversations complete with questions and answers, all without a recognizable word to be had! Fortunately, this level of babbling evokes a great response in most parents, who begin to feel a strong connection with their child. Most parents have had the experience of saying something to their baby and having the baby babble back in response, almost as if the baby understood what the parents said. If a parent responds back, a conversation begins between baby and parent. This motivates parents to speak to their child more often, which results in more practice for the child who will babble back. All this practice results in the coordination of the muscles around the baby's mouth and lips.

It seems accidental when a child puts two phonemes together and magically says a word. A parent's delighted response stimulates the baby to make more efforts and more syllables. Traditionally, the two phonemes that are the easiest to combine are "m" and "ah" which together make "ma." I have a personal theory, unsubstantiated, but highly plausible. Many eons ago, our ancient mother heard this first natural, spontaneous syllable and claimed it as an indicator of the child's recognition of her as mother. To this day, some variation of "ma" stands for mother in almost all languages, no matter what their origin.

Of course, father was not to be left out! The next spontaneous syllable is "dah." So it is highly possible the ancient father claimed it as his, hence the presence of "da" or "pa" for father in most languages. Parents assist this process by saying "mama" or "dada" or "pah" over and over to the child, stimulating further practice of this oft heard combination.

When a child speaks the first recognizable word, it is a seminal moment in time. This accomplishment reflects not only the physical maturation of the throat, mouth, and tongue, but also the fact that the child has generalized her experience into a symbolic representation. This first word stands for some object; something or someone!

From these first words, received with such great delight, a baby begins to expand her vocabulary, learning about fifty words by eighteen months old. This is as much a reflection of the slowly coordinating musculature around the mouth and lips, as it is a child's connection with the fact that things have names.

THE MAGIC OF WORDS

Once a young child reaches the threshold of fifty words, a magic seems to take place and his increased vocabulary takes on exponential proportions. Very quickly, the child expands his vocabulary to include a repertoire of primarily nouns, a few verbs, the word "and" as a helpful conjunction, plus a handful of essential prepositions such as "in," "on" and "up."

In *What's Going on in There?*, Dr. Eliot explains that children's brains are innately biased to assume three things about words:

1) They refer to whole objects, as opposed to their parts or properties;
2) they designate classes of items, rather than individual members of the class;
3) objects have only one name.[4]

Once a child reaches that milestone of about fifty words, he begins to add several words a day to his speaking vocabulary. However, the number of words he understands grows even more rapidly. Between the ages of two and six years, a child can learn a staggering eight words a day.

The primary dialogue between an adult and a child early in this stage consists of answering a child's number one query: "What's that?" The child's understanding that everything has a name stimulates his desire to validate everything he is familiar with by naming it.

During this time of increased dialogue with an adult, a child is also intuiting the structure of the language. Even a child's simple fused phrases always put words into the proper syntactical order.

It becomes obvious that the child has already intuited the syntactical order of the language. In other words, the child already knows unconsciously that different words function in various ways and that these groups of words have defined positions within a larger communication. No one has taught him this "grammar," but his brain is already using this knowledge.

By two years old, a child has intuited the complete structure of language and he can speak understandably. Indeed, what a child accomplishes in twenty-four months replicates what it has taken humans as a species tens-of-thousands of years to accomplish. Never again in the child's life will he have such ease and facility in learning a language. Learning a new language as an adult is far more difficult than during that golden sensitive period for language.

LANGUAGE, BRAIN GROWTH, AND CULTURE

For the next four years, a child's vocabulary expands from a couple hundred words to thousands of words. Childhood linguists know that by the time a child is six years old, she will understand between 10,000 and 15,000 words. Ten thousand words make up the everyday spoken vocabulary, meaning these are words that the child uses readily. The remaining 5,000 words are ones that the child recognizes and understands when used in context, but she may not use them in her everyday language.

Literally, everything that a child has experienced and recognized in the world must be labelled. This presents a great task for the adults who share the child's world. Precise, specific language is very valuable to a child developing her language skills. Parents who communicate with their child using baby talk are doing a great disservice to their child's language development! The parent who speaks with her child using the correct names for the objects of interest and the processes that they are carrying out, gives this child a great gift.

Dr. Montessori understood the need to provide a child with accurate information and specific names for people, places, and things in order to satisfy a child's hunger to learn. This is why she developed an extensive Montessori environment that encourages language development. Dr. Montessori used the technique of "the three-period lesson" in order to help children learn new vocabulary. Later on, Montessori guides developed the "sound game" to help children learn to hear all the phonemes of their language. (Three-period lesson and the sound game will be discussed later in this chapter.) Today, the Montessori classroom still incorporates these techniques.

Montessori teachers give vocabulary to name all the experiences a child has. A child in a Montessori environment learns the vocabulary associated with common activities, such as folding cloths, dusting a table, or arranging flowers. The child also learns the names of the tools used to carry out these activities, such as dusting cloth, vase, funnel, water pitcher, tablemat, and green bucket.

Teachers also use sets of picture cards for many different classifications of things, from a basic classification for "Living and Nonliving Things" to the more complex classifications for "Insects and Arachnids," and classifications for "Instruments in an Orchestra" based on sounds each instrument makes. These techniques and materials are specifically designed to nurture this sensitive period for language. The challenge for any Montessori teacher is to find or make enough sets of cards to correspond to the spontaneous interests of the children in her classroom. For instance, if a child is interested in fish, then a set of cards based on fish classifications would be very stimulating to that child.

During the sensitive period for language, a child also needs the opportunity to explore the nuances of language as a means to validating what is known and as a means of communication. The child has discovered that language is used as one tool for connecting with other humans and begins to practice communicating ideas and needs. This is a time when parents must practice tremendous patience in listening to their child talk and talk and talk, and answer what seems like endless questions. While a parent may crave moments of silence, the child is craving information about her wondrous world!

It is important to note here that a child who has limited language must struggle to be heard and to be understood. Often, out of frustration, this child will use physical force to communicate instead of words. Parents may worry about a child who doesn't speak much or who stutters. Patience is the key to helping this child.

If you are concerned your child has language limitations, the first task is to establish that there is no physical impairment. I had a little boy in one of my classes who didn't communicate much and seemed to not hear well either. When I mentioned this to his mother, she took him to a doctor who discovered scar tissue on the eardrums due to a series of ear infections. As a result, we all learned to listen carefully when Matty spoke, and to speak clearly when talking to him.

Another set of parents brought their three-year-old daughter, Jenny, to my classroom and expressed great concern that she only used her own sign language to communicate. After talking with the parents for a while, I learned that at home Jenny's ten-year-old brother did the speaking for her. Also, medical tests indicated Jenny had no physical impairment. So, in the classroom I decided to "play dumb" to Jenny's sign language and encouraged her to use words. For several weeks, Jenny resisted and attempted to communicate with signs. I kept acting as if I didn't understand what she was asking. Out of pure frustration one day, Jenny shouted out what she needed. "I want to work with the apple cutting, I can't find it."

I was delighted to hear Jenny speak with complete sentences and with a rich vocabulary! For the first time, Jenny *had* to communicate on her own behalf. Within weeks, she was talking with all the other children in the class. Her parents thought they were witnessing a miracle!

LANGUAGE, BRAIN DEVELOPMENT AND THINKING

The impact of learning a language as the key to the development of functional communication skills is tremendous.

However, what is more powerful is how language influences the development of the brain and the capacity for thinking. The evolution of the human species and the major development shifts that have resulted in humanity as we know it today, are directly related to language both as cause and effect.

In his book, *Origins of the Modern Mind: Three Stages in the Evolution of Culture and Cognition,* neuroscientist and psychologist Merlin Donald, Ph.D., looks at both changes in brain structure and the influences of culture on the development of language in modern times. He explains:

> Human culture, in its most basic manifestation, is an integrated pattern of adaptation, a complete survival strategy. It forms the larger framework into which various cognitive components of that culture, including language, must be fitted.[5]

Neurologist Frank R. Wilson, M.D., also gives us insight into the role of language. In his book, *The Hand: How Its Use Shapes the Brain, Language, and Human Culture,* he writes:

> Human language presupposes expressly cooperative relationships between people with a common encoding-decoding plan. In other words, language is prima facie evidence on an information-sharing life between people. When people created formal languages, they created mechanisms for sharing information, and in so doing authenticated the existence of mutual awareness and cohesive purposes in their lives. The word we use for that arrangement is "culture."[6]

Language appears to be unique in humans who seem to have a brain hardwired at birth for language development. Language acquisition is universal, hence the connection to a sensitive period that Dr. Montessori described some one hundred years ago. Despite the great diversity of differences from one spoken language to another, *all* children are driven to talk and *all* children develop language in a similar manner.

Spoken language is the foundation for social interaction. All languages are composed of sentences and use the same generic parts of speech, such as nouns, verbs, and adjectives. The order and organization of these parts of speech are clearly specified by rules called grammar. This applies to all languages.

The notion that language must have a structure is important. There is evidence that the absence of this structure will drive a generation of children to create it in order to fully develop a capacity for language. Linguist Derek Bickerton, Ph.D. explores in his book, *Language and Species,* the spontaneous creation of a language structure by cultures of children whose parents speak only a "proto-language." African slaves from different tribes and with different languages were found early in the twentieth century working on the plantations in Suriname, South America. The overseer for the plantation was Dutch. The adult generation of Africans spontaneously created a new vocabulary with words taken from the various African languages and some from the Dutch language. This is what Dr. Bickerton called a "proto-language" or what we might think of as the precursor to a new language.[7]

Dr. Bickerton studied the development of language skills amongst a variety of African slaves from a variety of different tribes. The Africans all brought different vocabularies from their cultures. As they were forced to communicate with each other, they arrived at a common vocabulary understood by all, and a reflection of words from all the original languages.

The tendency to create a new language or to re-shape an already existing language by adding words from other languages has been going on for eons. Early humans lived in isolated tribes. Each tribe created language that reflected the tribe's particular life and experiences. As each tribe came into contact with another tribe, the languages of both tribes were changed. This dynamic aspect of language goes on in modern times as well. For example, in the English language the words "taco, bisque, and pizza," are all common words among English speakers that have been taken intact from each word's original language, whether it is Spanish, French, or Italian.

Dr. Bickerton notes that the missing piece in the new "proto-language" was a structure into which the vocabulary could be used, thus limiting their powers of communication. The generation of children born to the African slaves spontaneously created a syntactical structure, as if the psyche knew that something was missing and must be created to compensate. This was the beginning of an entirely new language, created out of necessity by a culture of displaced, enslaved Africans and their children.

One might question how the children could create something that was not present for them to observe and imitate. Noam Chomsky, Ph.D., considered one of the fathers of modern linguistics, theorizes that language is so universal that it must be inherent in the human mind. This distinction is important because it implies that the development of a spoken language is not merely an imitation of language that is modelled for the children. That is not to say that the linguistic surroundings of other humans using speech to communicate are not important, but the creation of language goes beyond that.

Dr. Eliot addresses the same phenomenon that Dr. Chomsky advances. She asserts, "The capacity for language may be genetic, and our grammatical rules may be limited by the universal features of human brain hardware, but the particular language a child masters, and the way he ends up speaking it, are largely a function of experience...the very act of learning language is what directs the specialization of the linguistic brain."[8]

A child is going to learn a spoken language no matter what that language may be. He is going to build a vocabulary and intuit the structure of the language, whether his exposure is rich or limited. Even if it is true that the capacity for language is genetic, it is still essential that a child hears vocabulary in context. For instance, this means speaking with the child; having informal, spontaneous conversations about a variety of topics; or reading books to him.

Parents do not need special educational materials at home; they just need an awareness that naming things for the child is valuable in helping him to feel comfortable in the world. Looking at books and having the child name what he sees in the pictures can be a favourite activity for a young child. Taking a nature walk and naming all the interesting things a child sees can be a delight in any season.

Dr. Montessori fully understood the importance of these spontaneous moments as learning opportunities for children. One of her early followers, Margot Waltuch, related a story about the creation of the botany cards for the Montessori environment. One beautiful fall day in Rome, Ms. Waltuch was observing the children in one of the early *Casa dei Bambinis* playing in the crisp, fallen leaves. The children crushed and smelled the leaves, raked them into piles and rolled in them.

Ms. Waltuch was delighted with this full sensory experience and shared her observations with Dr. Montessori, who agreed that the children had had a wonderful sensory experience. However, she asked, "What could they learn about the leaves?" Scrambling for a nugget of wisdom, Ms. Waltuch replied that the children could learn the names of the kinds of leaves and the parts of the leaf. Dr. Montessori thought that was a good idea.

Ms. Waltuch then spent all night in the local library researching information on leaves and painstakingly making tissue paper drawings as the templates for card material. These drawings were the inspiration for the Leaf Cabinet, which still exists today in Montessori classrooms. Dr. Montessori knew through her observations that children delight in the richness of new words, especially when those words reflect their own new experiences.

As parents and teachers, we often forget the power of new words. A little five-year-old girl named Cathy reminded me of the impact of new words. She chose to trace the geometric figures in one of the drawers of the Geometry Cabinet. After some time spent tracing, Cathy asked for the names. A naming lesson was done with these figures—the oval, the ellipse, the curvilinear triangle, and the quatrefoil, which has four lobes or foils, often seen in a four-petalled flower.

Later that morning, Cathy climbed to the top of the jungle gym on the playground, looked down, and to her delight discovered a series of quatrefoils. She couldn't wait to share this discovery with everyone, including her grandfather who came to get her at school. What I found interesting was that Cathy climbed to the top of the jungle gym every day, but the day she learned the name of the geometric shape, she was overcome with excitement at being able to name a familiar shape. This is the power of language!

WORD USAGE, GRAMMAR RULES, AND PRONUNCIATION

The maturation of the grammar portion of language development is also important. There are two basic tricks to grammar—you create meaning by the order of the words or by changing the little bits added on to the words (the inflections). Toddlers begin to understand the differences in word order by about fifteen to eighteen months old.

Seeing Dad get ready for work, the toddler may say, "Me go?" The subject and the verb are in the right syntactical order even though an incorrect pronoun is used. The syntactical order will be accurate for the language that the child is learning to speak. For example, a toddler learning to speak Spanish would say, *"Te quiero,"* which is appropriate and syntactically correct Spanish when saying, "I love you." However, this would not be accurate syntactically when translated literally into English, which is, "You I love."

Another example might be a toddler reaching upward, asking, "Me up?" Here again, the subject preceded the preposition in the right syntactical order. No one has taught this order to this young child, it has been intuited along with the vocabulary, and is recorded in the brain at the same time.

Children between ages three and six are especially engaged in this aspect of language development. First, they intuit the differences in word usage, and then they begin to figure out the grammar rules appropriate to their native language. Most articulation errors are actually over-generalizations. For example, a child may say, "I ringed the bell," instead of "I rang the bell." This is an over-generalization as the child has applied a typical pattern in English for changing a present tense verb into the past tense. It is only later that the child will learn that there are numerous irregular verbs in English where this pattern doesn't apply. The child will memorize these irregular verb changes once he becomes aware of them. Another example of an over-generalization would be the child saying, "I have two foots," instead of "I have two feet." Again, this is an "exception to the rule" in the English language.

During the second half of the sensitive period for language, from age three to six years, a child will continue with three important processes; building a rich vocabulary, finalizing the pronunciation for the last few consonants, and applying the appropriate grammatical patterns.

It is not necessary to correct children's spoken language, as this tends to make a child feel inadequate or incompetent in his ability to communicate. The best approach is to simply restate what the child says, but with the correct usage. For instance, a child who says, "I ringed a bell," simply needs to hear you say in response, "Yes, you rang a bell!" The child's communication is validated and the child hears the correct verb usage without feeling guilty or self-conscious about saying something "wrong."

Language development and its capacity for higher thinking skills is a crucial connection. Early on in language development, we get so focused on the value of language for clear communication that we often forget the reciprocal impact that this development is having on other aspects of a child's developing intelligence. This essential connection brings us to the sensitive period for the development and refinement of sensory perceptions, which is discussed in the next chapter.

CHAPTER EIGHT
Learning Through the Senses

Dr. Montessori described a child's absorbent mind as constantly gathering an abundance of images from the physical world. At birth, a baby's senses are attuned and already have been absorbing information while in the womb. There is evidence that the brain has begun some embryonic sorting and discrimination before birth. Without going into complicated chemical descriptions, simply stated, the sense receptors in a fetus are "sensitive" to whatever information is present in the womb.

After a baby is born, the stimulation of the five sense organs becomes even more intense since these are the pathways for a newborn to gather impressions from the surrounding world. Each sense organ is primed with receptors that are stimulated by elements within the environment. One might ask: "What does it take to stimulate the sense receptors?" The fact is, nothing! Everyday living conditions provide sufficient opportunities for a newborn to begin absorbing his or her world.

The auditory receptors, olfactory receptors, and tactile receptors, especially for texture, are highly attuned to stimuli at the moment of birth. What does this mean for the newborn infant? Immediately, a newborn can recognize the sound of his mother's voice as well as other voices that have been a constant part of the baby's environment—even before birth.

On several occasions I have had the pleasure of an expectant mother attending my Montessori courses. During classroom time, the fetus heard my voice on a daily basis for several months. In each instance, once the baby was born, the new mother brought her infant to class for a visit. Oftentimes, babies will be fussy or anxious in an unfamiliar place. In my case, as soon as I began speaking, the fussy baby calmed down as if recognizing the sound of my voice and thinking, "Oh, there is something here that I know!" The mothers were always amazed at this reaction. The sound of a familiar voice is a known landmark for a baby, even if it is a lecturer!

The smell of the mother's body is another significant landmark at birth. Using a familiar blanket with the mother's smell can help a baby feel more secure, especially when a new person wants to hold the baby. The blanket carries the mother's smell and the baby responds as if his mother is still carrying him.

Another sensory response for babies at birth is touch. A baby's skin is extra sensitive, so the softness of a blanket, the sensation of water, or the change in temperature can all evoke an infant's response. Skin-to-skin contact is often very comforting to an infant, especially when she is stressed.

From day one, a newborn's eyes take in impressions related to shades of dark and light, shape, and dimension. Initially, the visual receptors in a newborn's eyes absorb the patterns of difference between the colors black and white. Within a week, an infant's eyes begin to see colors once the cones and rods in the eyes are finally aligned. So, an infant will respond to a simple black and white crib mobile before he will respond to a fancy multi-colored mobile.

Throughout a human's life, each sense takes in a discrete set of impressions. This holds true for the young infant, too. For instance, the auditory sense receptors in the ears absorb impressions of volume, pitch, and timbre. The tactile sense takes in impressions of texture, weight, and heat. In the case of the sense impressions for taste and smell, it is somewhat different from the other senses. Taste and smell absorb different categories of information, but not different qualities. For instance, a newborn's taste buds can distinguish between the category of salty or sweet, but this is all still the same sensation of taste. For smelling, the nose's olfactory receptors can distinguish a pleasant floral odor from a spicy pungent odor, but it is still the same sensation of odor. These are different categories of information, but are not different qualities of the physical world. All the information is for the same category.

While taste and smell are limited to a single kind of information, they are also the only two senses reflecting an intimate relationship with each other. Interestingly, the impressions taken in by the gustatory sense of taste and the olfactory sense of smell are most often used in tandem to distinguish one food from another.

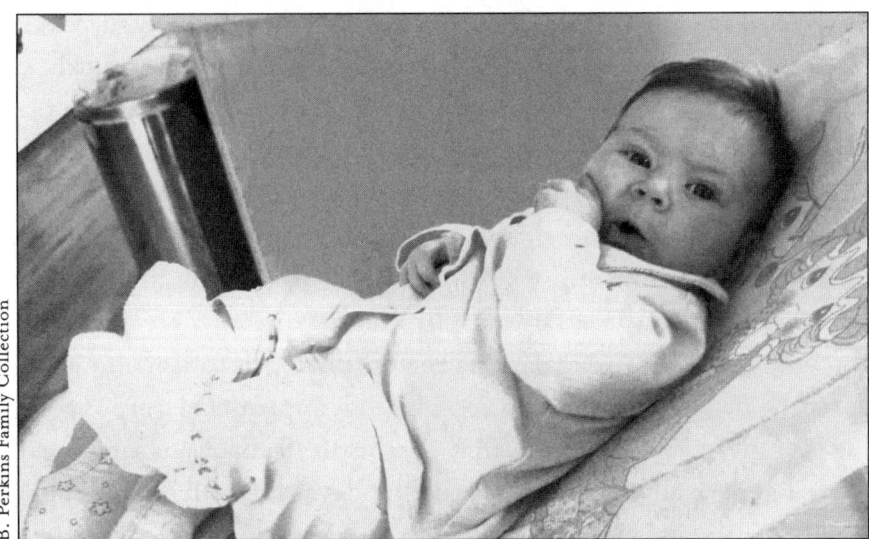

B. Perkins Family Collection

Newborn observing the world.

SENSORIAL PERCEPTIONS AND MOBILITY

While a newborn is virtually immobile for an extended period of time, the sense organs are still doing their work. In fact, there is some evidence that this extended period of limited mobility is designed by nature to allow the sense organs to carry out their initial explorations within the limitations of the body's position in space.

For example, how could a baby know what to reach for until her sensory responses have observed the object's position in space? This would be impossible for a newborn. The arm needs the eye to guide it through space toward the object. It is the eye that communicates the small adjustments that need to be made as the arm approaches the object. A good example is the child who sees a toy on the floor in front of her. Initially, she reaches out and hits the object with her hand, often moving the object away or sending it rolling. The child cries, mom brings the object back, and the baby reaches again, this time adjusting her hand to interact at a different point on the object or from a different direction. Gradually, the baby figures out what works most effectively and uses only that set of movements.

Babies are motivated to continue exploring with each success in touching and moving objects. It is amazing to see how quickly an infant becomes quite expert in successfully finding a toy or a play mobile and making it move. We are not speaking of days of activity here, but rather minutes! This is the amazing power of a baby's brain to interpret the signals coming in from the eyes and the skin, and communicating a response back to the muscles. Indeed, a newborn's brain activity is not simply one of absorbing and recording the sensory data. Its greater mission is to learn to interpret the data coming in and to define an appropriate response.

It is significant to note that the brain's capacity is not hardwired genetically. The brain must be developed through experience. While gathering impressions is essential, a child needs to organize this information into a useable whole within her brain.

PATTERNS AND REPETITION

A baby's brain records randomly, somewhat haphazardly, and without any intent to make the appropriate relational connections. In time, the brain begins to organize information according to patterns. The easiest patterns for a baby's brain to discern are patterns of similarity. Patterns that are repeated, over and over, tend to stimulate the same neural networks/cells. As the connection becomes strengthened, the pathway to this information becomes stronger. Stimulating the same set of neural cells repeatedly in babies and young children builds more synaptic connections between these same cells.

Repetition also facilitates the creation of a defined pathway in a newborn's brain, which leads to a defined network that allows for easier and more accurate use of learned information. Lack of repetition will result in unrelated neural connections in the baby's brain to eventually be dropped from the neural network. Brain cells must be stimulated in order to create the chemical energy necessary to become a fully protected neural cell.

ASSIMILATION AND ACCOMMODATION

A young child's new experiences and impressions are readily connected with his previous recorded experiences. The brain recognizes information with similar patterns and stimulates the neural network most closely related.

Swiss psychologist and philosopher, Jean Piaget, Ph.D., was an epistemologist who studied and wrote about the qualitative development of knowledge during the twentieth century. Two main concepts in Dr. Piaget's theory of knowledge development are the processes of "assimilation and accommodation."

Assimilation suggests that when a child is presented with new information that is a close match to information from previous experiences, then the child's brain readily accepts the information and connects with the neural network built from the original sets of sensory data. For example, a young child has a category of information related to the nature of a chair— what it looks like, how you sit on it, etc. I call this the "nature of chairness." Then the child goes into a new room and sees a new chair that looks similar but with differences. Although the child has never seen this particular chair before, he readily files this new information in the category for "chair," further defining the context of what can be included in the "chairness" category. The child might even climb up and sit on the chair, as if to verify that he knows what this is for.

Accommodation allows for a child to take in new information that doesn't fit quite so readily into an already established category. Staying with the example of the chair, the child crawls into the family's home office and finds this strange piece of furniture in front of the desk. There is nothing about its design that connects with "chairness," until Mom comes in and sits on it. The act of sitting upon this object connects it with the notion of "chairness" and forces the child to accept this information. The child's ability to accommodate expands the chair category to include this new experience.

As we all once experienced, this process of assimilation and accommodation is a significant part of a child sorting out new experiences so he can create accurate usable categories. Refining categorizations, or classifications, continues at a rapid pace throughout the first six years of life.

An important side note is that young children are not the only ones who have to "rethink" the classification for chairs—especially with the novel new computer chairs now available! I remember the good laugh my son's grandfather had when I saw his new computer chair for the first time. When Grandpa invited me to "sit" on the chair, I could not figure out what to do with my body. This new "chair" was one of those computer chairs that you actually kneel on instead of sit on, even though it still has a seat for your bottom. It gives "chair" a whole new meaning!

An even more dramatic example of adults challenged to assimilate and accommodate is the introduction of the computer and the Internet. Many adults have difficulty with this brave new world, whereas their school-age children (or younger) are very comfortable and proficient with the latest computer capabilities and software.

Another classic example of assimilation and accommodation is the four year old who goes to the zoo and sees penguins for the first time. You can tell the child that this species of animal is a bird, but there is little chance that he will believe you. There is very little about the look or behaviour of a penguin that fits with a child's or a layperson's classification for "birdness." It will take some later experiences and research before a child or an adult will readily redefine the classification to accommodate this unusual example of a bird.

SENSORY DATA AND CLASSIFICATIONS

During a child's sensitive period for the development and refinement of the sensory perceptions—from about newborn to age four or five years—the sense organs are essential for physical development. By its very nature, the brain is able to organize recorded information into broad classifications. These broad classifications are based on patterns of similarity—identification of what goes together or is related. However, the brain must be stimulated, we might even say "trained," to interpret the patterns of similarity and difference where the difference is quite small.

The brain can also be helped to distinguish one physical quality from another. For example, a child discovers an apple. Visually, the apple has color (red) and a shape (somewhat spherical). The apple may have a smell and it definitely has a distinct taste. As the child holds the apple, she experiences the weight and the temperature of the piece of fruit. Her brain gathers all these details and records them as raw data in order to learn how to distinguish color from shape, taste from smell, and weight from temperature.

All children have the ability to make these distinctions as they obtain more experience with these physical qualities in other objects. A child will see red on a book's cover, or will see the same apple shape in a rubber ball. A child will experience similar smells in other fruits and a similar taste in other kinds of apples. She may experience a similar weight in an apple and in an orange. The same temperature might be present in an apple and in a chilled cucumber slice. The brain begins to create these classifications separate from the objects themselves.

Dr. Montessori recognized from her study of Edouard Séguin's, M.D., work with the mentally disabled that sensory education was just that—education. This is education of the brain, not the sense receptors themselves. The eyes will see as well as the eyes can see, the nose will respond to smell as well as it always has. Sensory education requires challenging the brain to make discriminations between and among the sensory data taken in.

Dr. Séguin used sensory stimulation as the key to overcoming the limitations of mental retardation. While he was not successful in reversing this physiological limitation, he did discover the powerful impact that sensory stimulation had on the learning capacity of his subjects.

Dr. Montessori integrated many of Dr. Séguin's learning materials into her early work with the children and teachers at the Orthophrenic School (*Scuola Magistrale Ortofrenica*) in Rome. The results were astounding. At the end of the first term in July 1900, representatives from several Italian governmental agencies, including the Ministry of Education, visited Dr. Montessori's school. The visitors were quite taken with the children's ability to communicate clearly and to intelligently answer the adults' questions. Remember, these were impoverished children who had been housed in insane asylums prior to Dr. Montessori rescuing them from their awful surroundings and placing them in her educational program.

Perhaps the greatest indicator of Dr. Montessori's success with her "new method" was these deprived and illiterate children's metamorphoses over the next two years. Many of these children learned to read and write and even went on to pass Italy's national examinations given to "normal children" in the primary grades.

MATCHES, PAIRS, GRADATIONS, AND SEQUENCES

Out of curiosity, Dr. Montessori integrated these same materials into her work with children at the early *Casas dei Bambini.* Dr. Montessori wrote, "I wanted to experiment with the various methods used successfully by Séguin with children...but since we are constantly hampered by our habits and prejudices, I never thought of applying these same methods on pre-school children. The opportunity of doing so came to me by pure chance."[1]

Dr. Montessori was amazed to see how passionately the children were drawn to these materials, especially the children in the Casas who needed minimal adult intervention. The materials were simple and included items such as the early cylinder blocks, the touch tablets and the sound cylinders.

Children in an early Casa dei Bambini *(about 1912) working with a cylinder block and the sound cylinders.*

The children worked with the pieces of material repeatedly and loved the challenge to make matches among materials with small degrees of difference. In Montessori classrooms today, you will see children passionately working with many of the same materials. To this day, children love to match pairs of sandpaper tablets with five or six different degrees of roughness. Children are also drawn to the matching of colors, sounds, tastes, smells, and shapes.

With the materials used for matching, the child's brain readily sees the patterns of similarity. The common threads of a quality or set of characteristics stand out from all the information that doesn't match. In the same way that most people would remember a pair of twins at a party better than other new guests, the brain remembers the common threads or the matching threads of a sensory experience.

The ability to discern the patterns of similarity are reflected in the child's ability to make "matches" or pairs. A child, who can put together the two socks that go together, or who can sort the cans in the cupboard by some distinct quality, is manifesting this capacity to perceive patterns of similarity. Activities such as matching puzzle pieces to the outline of the shape, or putting identical pictures together support this training of the brain.

Dr. Montessori observed the activities of the children in the early Casas and took the challenge to a new level. She created materials

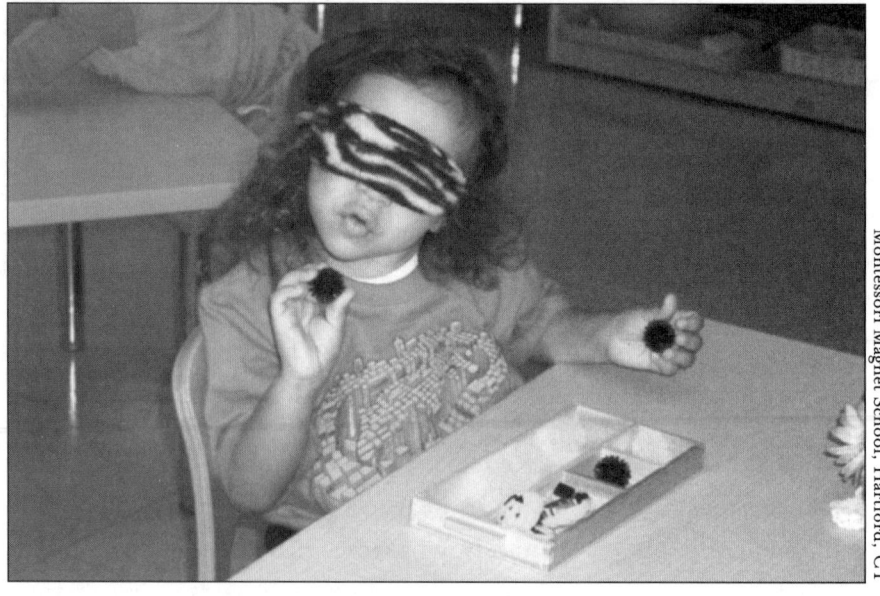

A girl sorts objects by touch.

that not only contained pairs, but materials that represented a gradation—a series with a measurable difference from one piece to the next. With this exercise, the greater challenge is training the brain to interpret differences within the same quality or characteristic. In the same way that a child uses discernment and discrimination to perceive patterns of similarity, he uses these same powers to interpret patterns of difference. The patterns of differences allow a child to refine the powers of discrimination to the point where small degrees of difference can be recognized. For instance, a child can readily perceive the difference between red and blue, but it is quite different to perceive the difference between two shades of the same red.

Montessori Magnet School, Hartford, CT

A girl grades the prisms of the Brown Stairs.

With increased discernment, a child can take a set of objects representing the same quality and put them in a serial sequence. In Montessori, we call this the ability to "grade values of a quality." This is the power that allows a child to grade shades of the same hue of the color red with the color tablets and to build the Brown Stair in order. The Brown Stairs is a set of ten rectangular prisms that differ in height and depth from one prism to the next. These ten prisms are a representation of objects that change in two dimensions. Typically, a child can place in correct order a set of materials such as the Brown Stairs around age three. At about three-and-a-half to four years old, a child's brain has developed enough to begin successfully grading qualities such as color, sound, or texture.

As a child's experience and knowledge increase, greater clarity is possible within these classifications. Since this developmental work is influenced by a sensitive period, we know that every human being develops these skills with some degree of accuracy during this early stage of life. The challenge for adults is to understand how to help this process be a little less random or left to chance, and to assist the process in a systematic manner.

Every child seems to have categories of sensory data that are particularly interesting to his mind. One child might be interested in colors and he becomes the master of the gradations of the color tablets, but shows little interest in the sound gradation represented by the bells. The opposite might be true for another child who can identify the gradation of the bells easily, but isn't very interested in the color tablets.

Adults can offer young children a richness of experience possibilities for every quality of every sense, and then allow the child to explore, in-depth, those aspects in which he is most interested. In essence, every day children are actively building an understanding for how the world is organized. They are sorting out what is related to what, and what is not related. They are training the brain to make interpretations and appropriate responses from the sum total of all the sensory experiences. Viewed from an adult point of view, this would seem like an overwhelming task.

ABSTRACTIONS AND GENERALIZATIONS

Again, we see the value and importance of the powers of the absorbent mind when a child learns abstractions and generalizations. The mind is able to carry out the organizational task of classifications without sapping the energies of the conscious mind. While the creation of classifications may seem astounding enough, it is not sufficient for the later learning capacities of the child.

The next step in building human intelligence involves the creation of abstractions or generalizations regarding things in the physical world and the nature of these things. Around four years old, a child begins to develop the capacity for abstraction. The foundational scaffold of classifications and categorizations developed in a young child's first years now expands to the next level with abstraction and generalization. As a child's capacity to learn grows, she continues to be inspired and motivated to explore the world and to create meaningful relationships with it.

The ability to abstract information is critical to a child's later development of thinking skills. The capacity for abstraction indicates that the mind can differentiate the essence from a variety of experiences. For example, a child has the ability to picture in her mind a bird and the qualities of "birdness" and discern those qualities that are different from a chair or "chairness."

These are indications that a child's mind has extracted the essence of this classification into a concept that distinguishes this information from all other information. At this level of abstraction, the child has developed the ability to access previously created information simply through the thought process. This is quite an advanced skill when compared to the earlier ability of the child to simply recognize something familiar when it crossed into the realm of present activity. In essence, it is one thing to recognize a chair, and quite another to see a chair with the mind alone.

Regarding abstraction, Dr. Lise Eliot notes, "Whereas recognition is automatic or reflexive, recall is by definition conscious...."[2]

The ability for abstractions is powerful in a child's mind. This will become the basis for the creative imagination and for thinking beyond the present moment and the limitations of the physical environment. But of what use is the abstraction in the mind if the child cannot readily access this information? The child needs a "password" or access code to retrieve this information and bring it into the conscious mind where it can be used. Language provides the key to this essential new capacity, which is memory. Dr. Eliot observes, "While language is not required for children to store conscious memories, it does play an important part in making memories last...."[3]

A child under the age of three cannot yet act upon recall. Researchers call this "deferred imitation," but it is evident that the more a child observes and records actions and behaviors, hears words, and listens to stories, the greater the possibility these recorded impressions will shape later actions. The more a child interacts with the physical aspects of the surrounding world and explores the dynamic that makes up this physical space, the more information the brain has to create abstractions.

LANGUAGE AND MEMORY

Building a capacity for memory is an ongoing life process that begins at birth. A child trains his mind to be able to hold information in the conscious mind as long as it is needed.

The first step is building the capacity to retrieve information from the mind's unconscious storage system. Language is the key to this retrieval system, which means a child needs accurate and precise vocabulary related to his experiences. For example, a child sorting out the distinctions of "redness" with the color tablets needs specific language; he needs the comparative and superlative language such as redder, reddest, less red or least red. The child can carry out the activity and can build the abstraction in his mind, but how can he bring this information into the conscious mind to describe the beautiful rose he just saw in the garden? The child needs more than just the word "red"; he needs rose, fuchsia, carmine, and burgundy. Later, the child will have the powers of discrimination to apply to all the different names for red crayons in the big box of crayons—cerise, magenta, maroon or scarlet.

The capacity of the mind to continue to build memory is associated with what is called "the elasticity" of the brain. It is quite evident that children's brains have great elasticity, yet this quality exists throughout life. For example, research today with Alzheimer patients focuses on keeping the mind stimulated so the brain will continue to make neural connections. Crossword puzzles, Scrabble, Sodoku, or any other brain stimulating activity along with aerobics or other forms of physical exercise all serve to keep the mind's elasticity. This is especially important with patients whose neural networks are breaking down.

Not long ago, the director of an Alzheimer's program on the East Coast contacted me. The director was looking at Montessori materials and techniques as one possible means to work with their patients. (Nothing came of this initial contact but it does reflect that others outside the Montessori teaching realm recognize the value of these techniques). There is one truism related to the brain that is easy to remember, "Use it or lose it." The brain systematically sheds unused brain cells from the age of three years until the end of life. So, if you're not using your brain for new and challenging tasks, the unused brain cells will keep dying off!

IMPORTANCE OF PRECISE LANGUAGE

Adults who use precise vocabulary when speaking with children create a context for them to absorb precise language to apply to their own experiences. This same language will be used later to retrieve the abstraction from the unconscious mind and to bring it into the conscious mind. As Montessori teachers, we look at the activities we offer in the Children's House to support this important work. Earlier, I mentioned a child's work in the Montessori classroom sequencing the Brown Stairs. It would be easy and typical for an adult to refer to the dimensional differences as big or little when in fact, the dimensional change is not large or small at all, it is thick and thin. It would be just as typical and easy to refer to the pieces themselves as cubes or blocks when in reality they are rectangular prisms. This precise use of language attached to a very precise set of information helps a child to fix this abstraction for two-dimensional differences in her mind. It also allows her the luxury of being able to use precise and accurate language in her own descriptions of objects she is exploring.

All of the pairing and grading work children do with the sensorial materials in Montessori prepares their minds to build abstractions. The moment we give children language, they gain the keys to verbal recall. Parents often communicate with their child using "baby talk." There is some evidence that the adult's high-pitched voice does stimulate the language center of the infant, however, baby talk becomes an obstacle to a child's development when parents continue to use the baby talk past the infancy period in a child's life.

Dr. Montessori observed how children love long complicated words. Parents recognize this when they hear their child name all the dinosaurs in a favorite book. Children love to roll difficult words off their tongue. It gives them a true sense of accomplishment in mastering challenging vocabulary. Children use these new words immediately as if they had known them all along. Cathy, a little girl on the jungle gym, shouts, "I see quatrefoils. I see quatrefoils." Daniel, a four-year-old boy, informs his dentist that at school he learned the difference between an "isthmus and a strait."

Given an introduction to the nature of compound words, the five-year-old children in my classroom went around for days informing me of new words they had just thought of—doorknob, chalkboard, or underpants. Often, parents think they must simplify their language so their child will understand. In fact, the opposite is true. Children will learn to communicate with a rich, diverse vocabulary reflecting the words they have heard. As parents, it is good to remember that we spend more time communicating with our children than anyone else. Parents are their children's primary language "material."

All the Montessori activities that engage the memory—from memory games with the sensorial materials to the applications of memory in writing, reading and mathematics—allow children to exercise these newly acquired powers. One of the techniques used in a Montessori classroom allows a child to explore how to formulate information into a cohesive context. This technique is a game commonly called the "question game." Children bring many treasures to school and want to talk about them. The Montessori guide can use the question game by asking a series of questions about the child's treasure. For example, if a student brings a locket to share, the teacher might ask, "Where did you get the locket?" "Who gave you the locket?" "Was the locket a gift for any special occasion?"

The child most often answers the teacher's questions with phrases that the teacher can then turn into a complete sentence. For instance, the child may answer the questions by saying, "My grandma, for my birthday party yesterday."

The teacher then responds, "Oh, I see, you got the locket from your grandmother for your birthday. She gave it to you yesterday at your birthday party."

By doing this, the child begins to see how to put thoughts together into a "story." The child practices telling her own story, and the teacher may invite the child to share her story with a classmate. This is a game that can easily be played between parents and their child.

Not only is this a support for the emergence and development of verbal recall and vocabulary development, but also it is a precursor to the development of creative writing and the capacity to communicate effectively with others, and enjoy it!

CHAPTER NINE

From Chaos to Order

The fourth sensitive period Dr. Montessori identified in child development is the development of order, which takes place from birth to about four-and-a-half-years old. This sensitive period is easy to miss or to undervalue because it has less discernible manifestations in a child's behavior and activities. Yet, the hidden ramifications of developing order are just as powerful as those associated with the sensitive periods for movement, language, and refinement of sensory perceptions. The sensitive period for order impacts a child's ability to create mental organization.

On a physical level, a child begins to sort out patterns in the external world at a fairly young age. Even a small infant is sensitive to the routine of the day. A certain comfort and security comes from the predictability of this routine, and a child expresses frustration when this routine is disrupted. This results in a feeling of dis-ease.

I remember taking a cross-country train trip with my son when he was only three months old. I thought being in unfamiliar surroundings or outside his regular routine wouldn't distress my infant son. Yet, we were barely on the train passing through one dark tunnel after another before he started fussing. It was difficult to calm him until we arrived at our destination and I re-established our daily routine. This experience was a great reminder to me of how early a young child can create a pattern of predictability.

A child takes great comfort in a daily routine and quickly begins to anticipate certain activities such as eating, sleeping, bathing, and playing. A child builds confidence knowing his self-preservation needs are responded to and there is a connection with another human being to assure survival.

MAKING SENSE OF THE PHYSICAL WORLD

An infant begins to sort out the parameters of the external world while also establishing a sense of self as separate from the world. It takes almost a full nine months for a child to begin to develop an ego—a sense of self as separate from the mother. This makes sense when one considers that a child was physically connected to her birth mother for nine months in the womb. The baby needs a commensurate period of time outside of the womb to separate.

During this time, the infant gradually discovers the extent of his or her body—the parameters defined by the extremities of hands and feet. When a baby discovers her feet, she is fascinated.

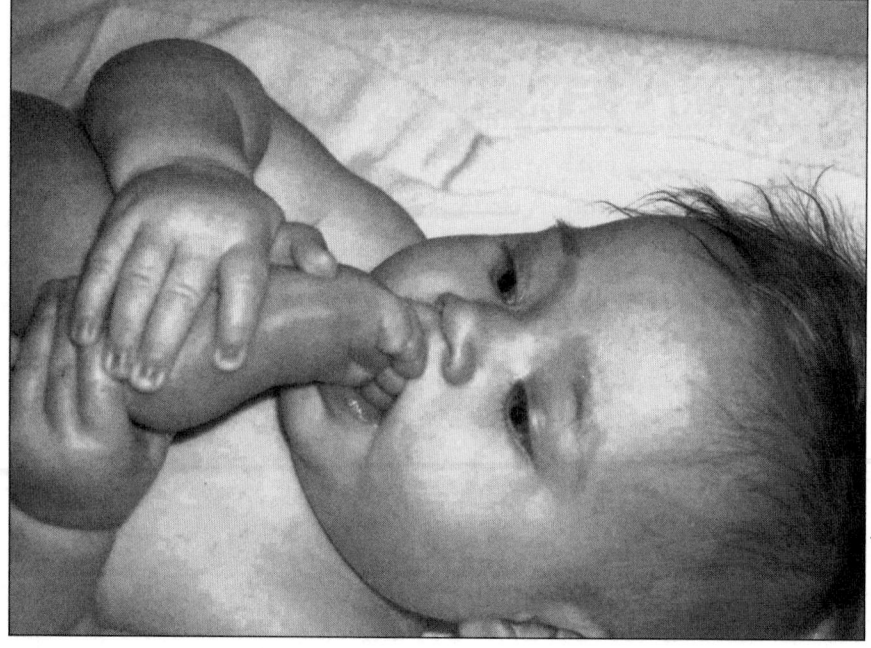

A baby orienting to her own body.

126

She explores these interesting objects and then cries when pain results after biting one of them. What a shock to realize that this "thing" is attached to her body!

As the various systems and organs of the body mature and become fully functional, a child intuits a sense of security and confidence that these functions can now be trusted. The baby is not consciously aware of the organs in her body, but manifests a feeling of comfort and security as all the systems begin to function appropriately. It is important to remember that the physical systems of the body are not fully functional at birth. In addition to the neurological aspects of the body, other bodily systems are still developing, such as the kidneys, and the digestive system. A child's sense of self is intimately connected with a beginning trust in her own body and its capacity to function independently.

During early infancy, a child sorts out familiar people and surroundings from those who are new and unfamiliar. As a child sorts out her separateness from her mother (or primary parent), there is a short period of disequilibrium generally called "fear of strangers." It is as if the child's psyche holds on ferociously just before admitting that it must let go. This process takes place whether the mother birthed the baby or adopted her. It usually takes place around nine to twelve months of age.

ROLE OF A PRIMARY CAREGIVER

A young child needs the security of continuity and predictability to depend upon while getting used to his environment. A relationship with a primary caregiver is essential for an infant's development during this sensitive period as the baby builds confidence in knowing that there is one person who is there on a consistent basis.

The primary caregiver, more than anyone else, is the one the child knows will respond to his needs no matter what. This experience is how a child builds a sense of basic trust and mutuality, the capacity to connect with other humans. Developmental psychologist Erik H. Erikson, profoundly influenced and reshaped views of human development. Erikson's theory of personality, the Eight Ages of Man, identifies the stages of development that span a human's entire lifespan. Considered one of the pioneers in the study of "life cycles," Erikson asserted that the foundation for trust and mutuality is established by the age of about twelve months. If a sense of trust is missing in a child's psyche, Erikson believed the child would most likely find it difficult to fully trust other humans in later years. The ramifications of this lack of trust in later social development can be tremendous.

EXTERNAL ORDER LEADS TO MENTAL ORDER

While a child is sorting out and establishing a sense of internal order, he is also gathering numerous impressions of the physical world that help him create a mental plan for relating to the physical world. In the process of taking in these impressions, a child inherently records information about the organization of the physical world and any links that exist in the presence and use of objects. For instance, even a very young child knows that a spoon is related to the act of eating, a pencil to writing, and a chair to sitting.

A child takes in the information about where objects are located and the predictability that those items will be in the same space. Based on his experience with external order in the surrounding world, the child will begin to create patterns of mental order. He gathers these impressions through the powers of the absorbent mind and integrates them into the very essence of his personality.

By the age of two, a child has built great confidence in the nature of the ordered external world. This is the height of the sensitive period for order. At two years old, a child becomes obsessive about order staying the same and not changing. This is a great reminder of the psychological security attached to the order of the external world. It may even seem as if the child is at odds with the external world because he is tremendously dependent upon it not changing.

Over the next couple of years, the child will begin to let go of the obsessive need for unchanging order, as he learns how to create order for himself. Parents see this phenomenon when they rearrange their child's room and the child becomes distressed. I remember moving into a new home when my younger sister was just about two years old. She went around the new house kicking the woodwork and declaring, "I want to go home. I don't like this house."

Dr. Montessori relates the story of a friend's two-year-old daughter who threw a tantrum while they were all getting ready to take a stroll in the park. The mother put her coat over her arm just in case she needed it. The daughter continued with her tantrum until the mother took the coat and placed it around her own shoulders.

In another situation, a two-and-a-half year old girl came with her parents to visit the Montessori training center one evening. There were many Montessori materials in the room and the child was very interested. She noticed that the pink tower (a sequential tower of ten pink cubes) was slightly out of order. During their visit, the little girl came up and whispered in my ear, "Can I fix your pink tower?" She couldn't stand to have the pink tower in disorder.

A child who has opportunities to explore activities where the order is dismantled and then recreated, soon learns strategies for creating order out of chaos. Each individual child seems to create the strategies that work best for her. Whatever the specific strategies are, the child will have created them through her own personal experience with exploring sequences, patterns of relationship, and the organization of the surrounding world.

Later on, the child will call on these individually created strategies when learning to read, to interpret numbers, and to carry out arithmetic operations. In time, these strategies will form the child's foundation for critical thinking, logic, an understanding of cause and effect, and the ability to reorganize reality with the imagination.

Montessori Magnet School, Hartford, CT

A girl builds a Pink Tower, learning sequencing.

A Child's Mathematical Mind

It is in this context that the work of the sensitive periods for order, and for the development and refinement of sensory impressions, provide the basis for the mathematical mind. The mathematical nature of the human mind is manifested even earlier in the work of the absorbent mind. It is the result of the interplay between the data gathering of the absorbent mind and the organizational powers of the sensitive periods. From a child's earliest experiences, she begins to build lifetime skills that will make it possible for her to perceive patterns, discern similarities and differences, and put information into sequential arrangements.

These growing powers of the mathematical mind are reflected in a young child's capacity to carry out activities involving one-to-one correspondence. For instance, the young child who helps set the table for dinner cannot quantify yet, so the child has to take one plate at a time to the table, whispering this mantra, "One for Dad, one for Mom, one for Grandma, one for Brother, one for me." Then the whole sequence is repeated for the forks, then the knives, then the glasses, and the napkins.

Does this take time? Yes, but the child is engaged in an activity that challenges her brain and builds a pattern of sequence and relationship. The fact that the table gets set, or some portion of it, is insignificant. What is most important is that the child could carry out the activity!

These powers are also reflected in the young child who is discerning patterns of relationships between things to things, things to people, and people to people. Dr. Montessori related in her writings a wonderful story of a young child, about two years old, who came into a room and spotted a needlework pillow depicting a child with a handful of flowers. The child marched over to the pillow, picked it up, kissed the image of the other child, and attempted to smell the roses. Dr. Montessori marvelled at what a wonderful manifestation of the child's understanding of the nature of each image and the proper response, even to just the images! This is the mathematical mind recognizing relationships that exist in the surrounding world and how to respond to them. When that young girl got a few years older, she understood abstraction and what images can represent.

MONTESSORI PERCEPTION OF THE MATHEMATICAL MIND

Generally, people might think the mathematical mind must only refer to some capacity of the brain to carry out arithmetic operations or to remember geometric formulas. This is not how teachers trained in Montessori consider a mathematical mind. To them, the mathematical mind is one that organizes data into usable patterns and builds the capacities to respond to patterns that exist in the world. This is an orderly mind, an organized mind. Montessori teachers realize that eventually, this will be the logical mind. The capacities of a person's mathematical mind will exist long after the powers of the absorbent mind have faded.

CHAPTER TEN

This Is My Family and My Home

Who creates the child's first environment?

Who has the greatest impact on the fundamental development of the child?

Where does a child first learn about the world and relationships?

It is the parents and it is in the home!

Clearly, the volume of self-help parenting books reflects how important this role is for parents. Unfortunately, most of these books do not provide parents with the day-to-day, common sense insights needed to assist the natural psychological development of a child. These books will give advice about handling specific situations. But the advice or strategies stated in one book are often contradicted in a different book, leaving parents to wonder what really is the right thing to do. A small sampling of parental questions would include:

- "Does 'time out' really work when disciplining my child?"
- "How can I get my child to cooperate when she is refusing?"
- "At what age, and how, do I help my child become more independent?"

Understanding child development from the viewpoint of Dr. Montessori's sensitive periods can be helpful. An understanding of the basic developmental nature of a growing child can help parents understand what techniques will work and at what ages.

Understanding how and when a child learns, and what he or she can learn spontaneously at a particular age, can help parents provide age appropriate activities and to be realistic in their expectations about their child's skills and behaviours.

Prepared Montessori Environments

Understanding the role of the sensitive periods in child development is important, however, Dr. Montessori was also concerned that educational materials support a young child's development. She spent the better part of her life creating learning environments that supported a child's educational development through the different sensitive periods. From the beginning when Dr. Montessori opened the first *Casa dei Bambini,* she developed and used materials and techniques for childhood education.

Initially, in the early 1900s, she focused her work on what is still called "The Children's House" environment for three-to-six-year-old children. Then in the 1930s, Dr. Montessori dedicated herself to creating a learning environment for six-to-twelve-year-old children. At each stage, Dr. Montessori used her observations of the universal needs of children as her guide for creating materials as learning aides and an approach that allowed children to learn as spontaneously as possible. In Montessori, these special environments are called "prepared environments."

The concept of prepared environments was quite familiar to Dr. Montessori. In her life as a physician, she saw many natural examples of environments designed to protect, nurture, and support the developing organism. From the bird's nest to the mother's womb, nature provides for the developing organism. Dr. Montessori realized it was important to pay attention to the surrounding educational environment, providing a prepared environment in a child's life from birth to adulthood.

Dr. Montessori recognized that the nature of the educational environment must change as the needs of the child changed. In her writings about the Four Planes of Development, she believed that an understanding of the intrinsic motivators, the natural patterns of development, and the child's ability for spontaneous learning were the keys to creating a suitable educational environment for a child. Indeed, she believed this knowledge should form the foundation for *all* education.

THE ENVIRONMENT FOR THE FIRST PLANE

The first environment for a newborn is the home and the close relationship with a primary care giver. In this first phase of life, parents have tremendous influence over their child's exposure to a prepared environment for stimulation and learning. In the subsequent phases, Montessori prepared environments that offer educational support from pre-school through high school.

Dr. Montessori always wrote about the mother as the primary caregiver as this was the normal assumption of her day. However, in light of changing roles in a new century and shared parental responsibilities in many societies worldwide, what is most important to remember is the role of a primary parent or caregiver that an infant can rely on daily. Today, it is often the mother, but can also be the other parent, a family member, or a primary caregiver.

Within a safe and nurturing environment called home, an infant begins to create a relationship to his world. Hopefully, the child can begin to perceive the world as an interesting place and a safe place with people who are supportive and loving. The newborn's initial bonding landmarks at the time of birth are the sound of the mother's voice and the smell of the mother's body. This initial bonding can also apply later to a father or other primary caregiver who is consistently present in the baby's life after the birth. For an extended period of time, the child views the world from this safe perspective. A child is totally dependent upon the primary caregiver(s) for all needs; food, shelter, clothing, warmth, and love.

Quite quickly, the other members of the family can become a part of this safe context. The infant learns to recognize the other members of the family and their voices, thus experiencing his first social environment. While the typical home is not designed for a baby or small child, it provides the essential elements—food, clothing, and nurturing. In the early months, a child will glean the first impressions about his home and what kinds of things make up his family's world. It is in the home that a child will first decide if his world is a safe, interesting place to explore and one from which he will learn the basics of human interaction.

In the earliest stages, a child uses his senses to perceive what is present. Parents often think they need to decorate the baby's room with all kinds of colorful and flashy designs to make it interesting. Remember, the whole world is new to a baby. He does not need external motivators to stimulate his attention. In infancy, brightness and cutesy in the baby's room are primarily for the excited parents!

Before a child can actually grasp or begin to move about, there is little need for much more than a play mobile above his crib or play space. A baby needs a nice soft blanket to define the play space on the floor and a safe place from which to view the world as it passes by. There is great value in placing your child in a child's seat on the kitchen counter and let him watch as you prepare dinner. This is a great time to talk to your baby while you are working. Tell your baby what you are preparing and what you are doing with the various food items. All this verbalization is stimulation for your baby's auditory discrimination, which he needs to develop language. Plus, the human connection with another person builds a sense of security.

Keep It Simple

It is safe to say that infants and toddlers are more interested in simple objects rather than the fancy toys with lots of bells and whistles. This holds true throughout a young child's growing years. All parents have observed with some humor that their young child is often more interested in the box a toy came in than they are in the toy itself. Parents note the young child who is fascinated by the corner of a blanket or the flexible tube of a vacuum cleaner rather than the slick toys. As adults, we might think, *What's the big deal about that?* Remember, for the young child, everything is new and worthy of exploration. A child does not take anything for granted.

In her earliest writings, Dr. Montessori described observing the children at the insane asylum in Italy who were so deprived of stimulating objects to explore that they scrambled to play with the dried breadcrumbs on the floor after a meal. Today, most children are not so starved for stimulation, but don't be surprised the first time you do see them exploring crumbs of dried bread, or the grit they find in the depth of the living room carpet! I can hear parents saying, "Oh, that's awful." Let me reassure you, it is okay; this kind of exploration is normal. Parents have to resist the temptation to judge the value of whatever it is that has captured their child's interest. Sometimes it is good to try to see the world through your child's eyes. When we do this, we are reminded of how interesting even the supposedly mundane items of life can be.

Helfrich Photo Collection

Fun Exploring Wildlife.

Another temptation for us as parents is to go overboard. We think that if a child needs interesting things to explore, more is better, and we go out and buy every item possible, especially if it is advertised as appropriate for building the intelligence of the child. A reminder: This is a good time to remember that less is better. A child who is already stimulated by the common items of the everyday world does not need a pile of toys or "educational aids" to keep her active.

Play with Your Child

Worldwide, parents play a delightful and simple game with their children called "Peek-a-Boo." This fun way of getting your baby to smile and giggle also provides numerous developmental aspects.

The child's sense of separateness from the rest of the world and the beginning of the development of ego are most obviously manifested in the pure delight that comes with playing "Peek-a-boo." A child uses this game as a validation that the object still exists even though out of sight, which is significant. Developmental psychologists call this "object permanence," an important stage of cognitive development for infants. Around eight or nine months an infant recognizes object permanence, which is a baby's essential capacity for the beginnings of memory.

"Peek-a-boo" also is an extension of social skills. The game requires interaction with an older child or an adult. A young child realizes this is one way to connect with another person. There is laughter and enjoyment exchanged between the baby and the other person. By playing this simple game, a baby learns the sense of playfulness, which is another important tool for connecting with other humans.

Movement for the Infant

As a child begins to crawl, more of her environment comes into play. In Chapter Six, I discussed the importance of removing barriers that limit a child's movement. Keep in mind that playpens, swings, baby jumpers, and walkers are obstacles to the development of a baby's movement as well as exploration. Even carrying or holding your child all the time can become restrictive and impede a baby's natural development.

There should be interesting items for your baby to practice grasping. A wooden rattle or a soft toy can intrigue a baby's natural inquisitiveness. A play mobile placed above the baby's play area, but within reach, becomes a stimulus for reaching out as well as for refinement of visual acuity.

Once a child can sit independently, parents can offer their child toys that stack, or maybe a small bag or plastic canister with a few common everyday items that can be taken out and put back in. These activities enhance a baby's refinement of grasping and build a sense of object permanence.

Around this same time, a child shows a preference for one object over another. Again, less is better! A child can only hold one object at a time in these early months of grasping and can only pay attention to one item at a time. Simple, everyday items are great toys. I watched a young child spend the better part of an afternoon exploring what could be done with an empty pie tin. Close by were numerous toys his mother had purchased to keep him occupied. The baby ignored these. What could be better than a pie tin and a wooden spoon?

CHILD-PREPARING A HOME

As your baby begins to move about, it is important to place those priceless heirlooms and sentimental valuables up high or inside a cabinet. Also, be sure to lock cupboards with cleaning supplies and other dangerous materials. Electrical outlets need safety covers. All of this is essential childproofing.

Items that come into your child's field of exploration should be items that she can touch, taste, and pick up. In addition, by putting valuables out of reach, you will limit the number of times your child has to hear the word "no."

However, once safety has been secured for your crawling and exploring infant, then you want to think about how to support the *development* of the child. There is a difference between childproofing a home and child-preparing a home. Childproofing meets the adults' needs. Child-preparing meets the child's needs.

Granted, there has to be a balance between the baby's needs and the rest of the household. A home must meet the needs of many humans, not just the new child. So, it is fine to close off an older sibling's room so the crawling baby can't disrupt or break an older child's toys, or worse, find small toys the baby can put in his mouth and choke on. Creating areas that encourage the baby's exploration can counterbalance blocking off certain areas of the home. For instance, create a kitchen cabinet for the baby that contains safe items, and provide an open space where your child can move freely. The music stereo or television with all the interesting knobs should be out of reach and replaced with an object that has knobs to explore.

Child-preparing includes providing a space within each room where your child can find items appropriate for exploration and supportive of your child's development. Is there a place in the kitchen where the baby can watch you prepare dinner? Even if you choose to feed the baby separate from the rest of the family, is there a place for the baby while you are eating so he can observe the social interaction of the meal and feel a sense of being included? In the living room, is there a special blanket for the baby on the floor? Are there simple, yet interesting, objects the baby can explore, such as a wooden ring, a cloth picture book, a ball, or a rattle?

As your child begins to crawl and eventually walk, more of the home environment comes into view and stimulates the baby's interest. Your crawling child needs open space to practice movement without running into the corners of furniture at every turn. On the other hand, a child delights in finding solid furniture that is useful for pulling himself upright. There can be a low shelf with his toys on it so he can crawl over and explore.

Once a child begins to walk with confidence, there can be simple items to stand behind and push. A simple cart with a tall handle in the back becomes a push cart and is great for transporting toys that the child finds too difficult to carry while walking. A pull toy on a long tether, especially one that makes a sound, is pure delight for a child just beginning to walk.

Toys, Toys, and More Toys

The key consideration when choosing toys for babies and toddlers is simple. That means, keep it simple!

Simple toys such as a soft cloth ball, a wooden rattle, a soft doll with no accessories the baby can choke on, or a toy on a string to pull are great options. Simple items with common, everyday applications are great for your child's early development of grasping and fine motor control. This might include items such as a wooden spoon, a metal pie tin, a plastic cup, measuring spoons or a bowl. Cloth books are also great for a baby to discover, which often involves tasting and chewing as well as looking.

By eighteen to twenty-four months, simple items might include clothing with simple fasteners (snaps, large buttons, Velcro); simple puzzles with pieces for matching, and a cloth or plush toy for cuddling.

The organization of your child's toys often becomes a challenge. Toy boxes require "dumpster diving" and usually result in every item out on the floor in chaos when your child is just searching for one particular object. A better option is a small, low set of two shelves with space for each item. This makes it much easier for your child to find the desired item and easier to encourage the notion of putting one thing away before taking out another. Even if a child gets several toys out at once, it is easier for the child to help put things away when she knows where they go. This is not some parental fantasy, but a reality that many Montessori parents experience with their children when parents take the time from the beginning to show their child how to put away a toy in the same place, on the same shelf. This can be the child's first experience with personal responsibility. In the Montessori Children's House, a child learns quickly to put back one item before taking out another one, and to clean up his workspace.

Most of us know all too well the phenomenon of too many toys and how easy it is for this to get out of control for a child. If we remember that a small child can only pay attention to one item at a time, or as they get older, just a few items at once, lots of toys are not necessary. When toys arrive in large batches, such as birthdays, observe which ones your child is interested in the most and substitute these for items on the shelf that the child is no longer playing with. Take the rest of the new toys and put them in a box on your closet shelf. Over time, other toys can be rotated on to your child's shelf to replace toys your child has outgrown or lost interest in.

Rotating a child's toys maintains an element of novelty and interest over a much longer period of time and usually results in real exploration. In addition, your child is less likely to become overwhelmed and just destroy the toys. A few new things of interest with increasing levels of challenge and age appropriateness keep your child exploring.

Remember, young children do not enjoy toys that do everything at the touch of a button or the flip of a switch. Things that are out of their control intimidate most young children. They do best with toys that are interactive and open to manipulation.

In addition to cloth books, you want to provide many storybooks that you can read to your child daily. Early childhood educators have recognized for many years that children who are read to are much more likely to learn to read themselves. It is not enough that our children see us reading for our own purposes, but they need to be participants in the joy of this activity. Your child also comes to cherish this special time with a parent.

PARTICIPATING IN FAMILY ACTIVITIES

Children should be allowed to participate, or at least be present, during family gatherings, including meals. The child's functional independence grows as she is offered simple choices and the opportunity to carry out simple activities for herself. A nine-to-twelve-month-old child has enough coordination to pick up small strips of cheese, small bits of soft meat, and soft vegetables or fruit. Put these foods on the child's tray while the family is eating and your child gets to join the meal. It is okay to supplement these finger foods if you feel your child is not getting enough nutrition. Also, respect the moment when your child indicates she doesn't like a particular food or is full. Do not force your child to eat something she doesn't like.

A child between one and two years old enjoys practicing with a spoon and even a small fork. It isn't always neat and tidy, but the child enjoys the experience. When the spoon doesn't cooperate, the fingers or fist do just fine!

At this same age, your child is capable of feeding herself. She knows which foods she really likes, which foods are okay, and which foods she doesn't like at all. Your child also knows when she has had enough food. Often, as parents we think our child doesn't eat enough at meal times. Remember, your child has a small stomach, which only holds a small amount of food at a time. It is much healthier for your child to eat small meals more often than to be forced to eat too much at three meals.

Remember, food is for nourishment, not for punishment or reward! Often, it is easy for parents to get into a power struggle with their child over food. Forcing your child to eat once she has indicated she doesn't want any more is a violation of body space. Using food to reward a child for "good behaviour" is just as destructive. The child who learns to use food as a reward often ends up obese or addicted to food. In the same vein, depriving a child of food as punishment also leads the child to experience food as much more than just nourishment.

Around this same age (one to two years) a child is ready to sit at the table using a booster chair. Children enjoy being able to serve themselves like the rest of the family and to participate in the spirit of the communal gathering.

By three years old, a child is quite competent at eating and now enjoys the opportunity to help prepare the meal. Children love to wash and peal vegetables, and cut them into pieces for the salad. (Be sure you watch closely any activity that involves cutting.) They also love to set the table and empty the dishwasher. (Of course, by the time they are teenagers this will pass!) If nothing else, your child will enjoy sitting and just visiting with you while you fix dinner.

As your child grows, she can do more tasks to help around mealtime. She can use a knife to cut her own food and will enjoy serving others. The adult who ignores these opportunities in effect controls all aspects of the child's life and robs the child of the practice necessary to build her will.

B. Perkins Family Collection

A young child really enjoying blueberries.

A child's process of "self-construction" is often messy and inefficient. Children need to be free to carry out their own activities as best as they can without restrictions or interference. For instance, pre-schoolers putting on their jackets and zipping or buttoning them up need time to practice this basic life skill. Most importantly, adults need to stand back and have the patience to give their children the space to learn these skills. Parents need to develop an attitude of "friendliness with error." This means allowing your child the opportunity to learn through natural, spontaneous "errors" or "mistakes." Messes are a part of learning. Don't be afraid of them!

LANGUAGE, SONGS AND BOOKS

A child's participation in family activities allows him to absorb spoken language. The richer the spoken language of the environment, the greater the child's capacity to create his own "mother tongue"—the child's first spoken language or languages.

While there is some evidence that an adult's elevated tone of voice draws a child's attention because the sounds fall into a more readily heard range of pitches, it is also important for a child to hear clear speech and distinct vocabulary. As parents, it seems natural to talk in "baby talk" to the baby. While this seems cute and somehow is meant to reflect the early speech of the child, it doesn't help your child hear natural human speech. A child hears the sounds of vocal speech and distinguishes these sounds from all other sounds within the first few months of life. In these first few months, a baby responds differently to human sounds than to any other sounds. An infant will turn her head toward a human speaker and the brain responds to human speech with excited neural activity. So, distinct, clear pronunciation of words is important, even during the early months of a baby's life. Your baby is listening!

A number of years ago, I had the pleasure of listening to a fascinating lecture by Magda Gerber at a Montessori conference for trainers. Ms. Gerber was an elder woman who had spent her life working with very young children. She advocated speaking respectfully to an infant whenever interacting with him or her. Even if the parent was only describing what he was doing as he changed the baby's diaper or gave him a bath. This recommendation is even more important in today's world because a baby is bombarded with sounds from many sources.

I was recently in a home where a posted schedule listed "language hour" and "movement hour," along with several other similar tasks. All of this was outlined for a nine-month-old baby! This parent needed some help understanding that language or motor development do not happen at set times of the day. These aspects of development are "life" for the very young child and continue throughout the day. Fortunately, the mother had just hired a young Montessori trained woman as the baby's nanny. I trusted that the nanny would quickly abolish the "learning hours" and replace them with warm human interactions throughout the day.

Parents have asked me if their baby listening to a CD or watching a DVD is a helpful way to increase language skills. The answer is, "No." Your child needs to see your mouth forming the words. His ear needs to hear the vocabulary that you use in your everyday life.

Around six months, a baby begins to physically practice all the sounds needed for any language. Your child will begin to imitate the speech patterns and vocabulary that he hears from you. We have all had the experience of visiting friends and listening to their child, who seems so precocious, use such "adult vocabulary." This child is most often not truly precocious, but is a child who has heard adult vocabulary and clear speech. This is the pattern that this child has learned as normal speech.

Your child can sound just as verbally smart, if you talk with him from the beginning, and allow your baby to listen to natural conversations within the family. This presumes that we take opportunities to speak with our children and not just at our children. Your baby is not going to talk back or carry on a conversation, but if you watch the body language and the mouth, you will see your baby responding to your conversation. By the age of two years, your child can begin to carry on a conversation.

By age three, your child delights in sharing his or her discoveries, delights, and needs. Your child begins to tell little stories about her experiences and interests. In addition to spontaneous conversations, good children's books, poetry, and songs stimulate language development. Children love to be read to, they enjoy singing songs with others, and learning simple poems or rhymes. Your child will enjoy nursery rhymes and little ditties as much as you did growing up! Some parents say they don't sing well, or they don't know any children's songs. It really doesn't matter. Your child enjoys the energy of you singing to them. They don't know you may be singing out of tune and they don't know that the rock and roll song that's been stuck in your head for years is not necessarily a children's song. Your child just loves hearing your voice and watching you sing. Often, parents will sing to their baby while he or she is still in the womb. One father I know used to sing "Take Me Out to the Ball Game" for his unborn child. Within the first half hour after the baby was born, the ecstatic new father sang his new daughter the familiar song. She gazed at him knowingly, recognizing the sound and finally seeing the person who sang her the song. Now, she is an adult, and loves to sing along!

I remember my Sunday afternoons as a young child when my father would let me help choose the records to stack on the record player. (This was long before CDs!) I didn't know all the names of the songs, but I recognized the record jacket or the color of the record label and knew my favorites. I was blessed with parents who loved a great variety of music from contemporary songs to show tunes to classical music. They passed on their love of music, which I, in turn, shared with my son. To this day, we all continue to have a great love of music.

On the other hand, I was not exposed to very much poetry when growing up. As a young Montessori teacher and mother, I used to think the poem about a patriot from the American Revolution,

"The Midnight Ride of Paul Revere," by Henry Wadsworth Longfellow, was good children's poetry because it was the only poem I knew. As an adult, I discovered the wonderful world of beautiful children's poetry from fellow teachers. There are excellent anthologies of children's poetry that will delight your child. For example, in the English language there is the classic by Robert Louis Stevenson, A Child's Garden of Verses, or the anthology by contemporary poet, Jack Prelutsky, The 20th Century Children's Poetry Treasury. If poetry is not your strength, remember, when all else fails, simple nursery rhymes will work, or a spontaneous rhyme you create on the spot.

Good children's books abound. When I was a young teacher in the 1970s, it was a challenge to find good literature in the United States that was appropriate for young children under the age of six years. That is not the case today. Entire bookstores are dedicated to children's literature.

Children under the age of two can enjoy simple stories and picture books. Your children will be delighted with just looking at pictures and naming objects in the pictures as you read them the story. Parents often forget that their child doesn't know the names of even some of the most common objects that surround them in their everyday world. Simple picture books organized around a theme such as farm animals, animals in the zoo, trucks, things we find in the kitchen, things we do to get ready for bed—all of these are great for very young children.

Looking at the pictures and naming the objects readily leads to little conversations about the objects or the animals. Your child is interested in the true details of the objects as well as the correct names. At any age, your children delight in hearing your voice as you read to them.

True stories or books about real things and real experiences that a child can relate to are important for children under the age of six years. These young children do not have the mental maturity to tell the difference between what is real and what is fantasy.

Fairy tales and folk tales with allegories are beyond the understanding of a young child. Their brains have not yet developed to the point to think in the abstract or to grasp the lessons offered through symbolism. In addition, the notion of trolls and elves, especially those that represent evil, young children believe are real and this creates fear within your child. These books are perfect for the child between the ages of six and twelve years old. By that age, children are developing a code of ethics, they begin to comprehend the difference between "fantasy and reality figures," and these tales fascinate them.

If you are fortunate to have a library in your community, you want to take your child for a first visit when she is about three years old. Hopefully, there is a children's section with an interesting selection of picture books and simple books you can read to them. My parents took me to the local library for the first time when I turned five years old. This was a rite of passage in my life. To this day, I remember getting my first library card. Children love books, so any way you can nurture a love of books will result in a lifetime gift for them.

CLOTHING AND INDEPENDENCE

When you think about child-preparing your home, keep in mind the importance of supporting independence around clothing. At age two, a child can choose his own clothing when you offer simple clear choices between two things. For example, you could ask while holding up two shirts, "Do you want to wear the blue shirt or the red shirt?" Then you can ask, "Do you want these gray pants or the brown pants?" As a parent, you will enjoy watching your child's decision-making process as he chooses.

One young mother I know helped her three-year-old daughter make this choice each night before going to bed and would then hang an outfit on the doorknob in readiness for the next morning. She relates the story of hearing rustling in her daughter's bedroom one night after tucking her in. When the mom went to investigate, her daughter simply said, "I changed my mind." Knowing that whatever was hanging on the doorknob in the morning was the only option, the little girl was attempting to make the switch. Her mother helped her make the change and all was well.

At a very young age, our children are capable of understanding the nature of choices and the responsibility that goes with making choices. Choosing clothes is only the first step.

Your young child can dress independently when clothing choices are placed where he or she can reach them. Even a child at one-and-a-half to two years can put on most pieces of clothing, including underwear, socks, a simple pull over shirt, and pants with elastic waistbands. Additional items such as shoes and outdoor wear are more complicated and require a bit more coordination. Around age three or four, a child can tackle the more complicated clothing.

By two years old, children can begin to learn how to take care of their outerwear when they remove it. You will need to have some low clothes hooks for hanging up jackets since regular clothes hangers are a mystery to many young children. You can show your child how to put his mittens inside his hat and then put his hat inside one of the jacket sleeves before placing the jacket on the hook. I have children put the scarf or muffler in the other sleeve. This system doesn't totally eliminate the desperate "I can't find my other mitten" panic, but it certainly does reduce the instances of lost or misplaced clothing. Just the idea of having a place for your child's belongings is significant. This stimulates a sense of personal responsibility, organizational skills, and independence for your child.

Between ages three and six, most children master the variety of fasteners found on clothing and become adept at getting into and out of most articles of clothing, including long underwear, snowsuits and mittens, rain slickers, and even jeans with snaps at the top!

Your child can also learn how to take care of his own clothing and items used throughout the day. As soon as your child is able to dress and undress himself, he can place his dirty clothes in a laundry basket at day's end. Your child can bring this laundry basket to the laundry area on a designated laundry day. By age five or six, your child can actually help sort clothes into whites and colors for washing.

Between three and six years old, children are usually fascinated by the art of folding and they love to apply this to clothing. If some clothing items seem too complicated for your child to fold, he can practice with dishtowels and bath towels. At this age, children can also put their own clothes into drawers and begin to learn organization in the drawers. This is a great way to allow your child to feel like a contributing member of the family community.

Learning Personal Hygiene

For starters, a simple stool in the bathroom allows your child to reach the sink to wash her hands and face. This builds a sense of dignity, competency, and independence in your child.

She can hang up the washcloth or bath towel on a low bar when done.

Your child can also start brushing her own teeth around age two. Granted, children need adult help brushing, and to be sure, parents will have to watch so all the toothpaste isn't squeezed out of the tube in a matter of days or minutes! The child who just chews on the toothbrush with a bit of toothpaste does an adequate job for most days and your child will find this a less intimidating experience than you taking the task vigorously into hand.

Bathing does require more adult attention for safety reasons as well as for hygiene. Until age six, your child probably needs a bit of help in the bath, especially to thoroughly wash her hair and to effectively use a soapy washcloth. The trick for parents is to only give the help that is needed and to let your child do the rest. When my son was seven, he declared his right to take a shower and to "do it myself." With a quick lesson on how to control the water temperature of the shower and a few chosen words about thoroughness, he took over quite competently. This was simplified by the fact that his hair was short and needed little care. As a child, my hair was long, thick, and braided every day until I was ten years old. I knew that I needed my mother's help. Depending on the specifics of your child's situation, she or he may also need additional help.

OUTDOOR ACTIVITIES AND INDEPENDENCE

In addition to the indoor environment, a young child needs a safe, secure yard where she can come into contact with nature on a small scale. Even an infant enjoys a ride in the stroller or in a baby backpack attached to your back in a position where she can see the world around her. Taking a walk through the neighborhood to see, feel, and smell the flowers puts your child in touch with the natural world. A ride through the local park offers your child fresh air, colorful images, and the excitement of other young children at play.

Once children can move about, a safe yard with both natural and cultivated spaces is ideal. Natural spaces are left a bit wild and attract natural wildlife that is appropriate to the size of the space and the nature of the grasses or bush. A small "wild" space that attracts a selection of insects and birds is sufficient.

The cultivated spaces are the green grassy areas that attract a natural life of their own. A young child between age two and six years can spend long periods of time sitting in the grass watching an insect at work or sit on the sidewalk watching an ant moving a crumb. These children enjoy beautiful flowers and can learn to look but not pick them. Pathways in a garden help a child reach all points in the garden without spontaneously walking through the plants and "becoming one" with the garden. Yes, on occasion, a young child will sample the leaves or the flowers or tempting berries, so give some thought to the kinds of plants within your child's grasp.

Part of the yard should be available and open for your child to play with large toys for gross motor movement and coordination. This could include a wagon, a push toy, or a tricycle, and a sandbox for digging and molding. If a secure yard is not possible, the local park is fine. The public park is not as supportive for independence because a child cannot come and go at will, but it is better than being confined to the house or an urban jungle of concrete.

SOCIALIZING YOUNG CHILDREN

It is natural for a parent to expand his or her child's social environment within the context of carrying out daily activities. Trips to places like the post office, the grocery store, the gas station, or the dry cleaners can be shared with your child. All a parent must do is pay attention for signals from your child that he is tired, hungry, or over-stimulated. With some thought given to the timing of these everyday excursions, your child can begin to expand his vision of life in the surrounding world. Your child sees other adults carrying out a variety of tasks, he sees the interactions with his parent, and he feels an accepted part of the on-going life of the larger community.

Shortly after adopting my infant son, I realized that the everyday tasks of life were still calling and necessary and had to be done during the business portion of the day. I would put my baby's car seat in the car and off we would go. Thomas seemed to enjoy our daily excursions to the local grocery store where the checkout clerk became a favourite because she always took time to pay attention to Thomas.

As Thomas grew, she was the source of many lollipops. Years later, the grocery store clerk would tease Thomas about "marrying her" and both delighted in his protests. Certainly, this was a connection forged over many years that he continued to enjoy well into his teen years.

Short excursions, again within the context of the family unit, can be expanded to include the zoo, the park, and the children's museum. Your child can expand her view of the larger world but again within a context where your child's individual needs can be met as they are manifested. A trip to the zoo doesn't need to be an all-day event. A couple of hours and a visit to just one part of the zoo are usually sufficient for a young child. Visiting only one limited part of the zoo keeps the stimulation manageable and allows the child the luxury of going slow and taking in all that is available.

Wherever you take your young child, keep in mind that children are not into many different experiences, but rather they are happier to take time to really explore one or two things. Adults must learn to set aside their agenda of "seeing all that we can manage to squeeze into the time available."

You'll know when your child is ready to move on, he or she will no longer be interested in watching what is present. I guarantee that you will be ready to move on long before the child is! Long, all day outings are usually recipes for frustration with most children under the age of six years. The day is too long, there is no way to take a nap, and after several hours the child has had enough stimulation. A trip to a theme park is a prime example of too much for too long. I think about all the children whom I observed having "meltdowns" at places like Disneyland. I have watched well-meaning parents drag their children through a long day at Disneyland, bound and determined to keep pushing in order "to get their money's worth." Short excursions are a much better alternative for young children, especially those under the age of six years. Save the expensive theme parks for when they're older—then they'll run you ragged!

EXPANDING THE SOCIAL CIRCLE

The extended family of grandparents, aunts, uncles, cousins, and the neighborhood community are important for a child before the age of three. Children begin to perceive themselves as part of the larger whole of humanity. They build trusting relationships with others beyond the initial intimate community of the immediate family.

After age three, a young child benefits from the expanded social circle with a small group of similar aged children. Whether this is school, playgroup, or just a social group of parents and children doesn't matter. What matters is that the child has the opportunity to interact with other children to practice social connectedness. It is within this context that a child will learn the words and behaviors that define what Montessori teachers call "common grace and courtesies." It is here that a child will most definitively experience connecting with others without mother or father having to be visibly present. This becomes another conquest in your child's growth toward independence.

CHAPTER ELEVEN
This Is My Montessori School

At around two-and-a-half to three years old, a child begins to feel limited by the parameters of the home environment. Dr. Montessori saw this as the point where a child moves into the second phase of the First Plane of Development. This transition calls for a new environment for a child's ongoing development and learning. At this age, a child needs an expanded social group of similar aged peers. Now, your child is ready for the Montessori environment in the Children's House!

CHILDREN'S HOUSE

Since the beginning, the first Montessori environment has been called the *Casa dei Bambini* or the Children's House. This environment, unlike a child's home, is specially designed to provide for children's developmental needs from ages three to six years. Dr. Montessori designed the activities in the Children's House to support the natural work of the sensitive periods in this phase of the First Plane and to support the ongoing work of the child's absorbent mind.

In the Children's House, Dr. Montessori organized the activities into four groups: Practical Life, Sensorial, Language, and Mathematics. Other activities related to culture and science (art, history, music, geography, botany and zoology) are integrated into the original four groups of activities Dr. Montessori first developed. She designed each group of activities to meet specific needs within a child's developing psyche.

Since then, Dr. Montessori's empirical understanding of children's development has been validated by current psychology and educational theory. A Montessori environment's special learning materials and the activities carried out with them attract a child's attention. These materials and activities also lend themselves spontaneously to repetition, which is essential to a child's brain developing neural pathways for continued development. Montessori materials build learning through a series of challenges that are age and skill appropriate.

PRACTICAL LIFE

Almost all educational programs recognize children's need for movement as a natural part of their on-going development. However, most educational systems isolate physical movement from the rest of a child's activities. Most standard schools provide special gym programs or unstructured play periods, providing children time to practice movements newly learned or discovered, but this playtime, in essence, is *random* practice. Traditional schools do not directly relate physical activity to specific intellectual activity. In this key approach, Montessori education differs.

Dr. Montessori viewed random activity as a misunderstanding of the role of movement in a child's development. In her book about the Montessori materials and their use, *The Discovery of the Child*, Dr. Montessori noted, "One of the most important practical aspects of our method has been to make the training of the muscles enter into the very life of the children so that it is intimately connected with their daily activities."[1]

These activities are found primarily within the context of the Practical Life exercises. The first thing to understand about the Practical Life exercises is that their aim is not the utilitarian end result, but rather to support a child's *total* development through interactions with a prepared environment.

In the Montessori classroom, the emphasis is on "life" and building life skills. For example, in Practical Life exercises, a child might appear to be learning to peel a carrot, but in reality he is also building a capacity to work uninterrupted, experiencing a sense of independence by doing something for himself, and learning a sense of sequence as he carries out the steps in the task. The carrot will get peeled as well as the child's skill allows, but the other parts of the learning experience will be much more important than the end product of a peeled carrot.

In Practical Life exercises, you might observe a child scrubbing a table repeatedly and wonder what it takes to get that table clean. However, the purpose of scrubbing the table is not to get the table clean, but rather the scrubbing is a response to a child's internal need to practice coordinated movement. Scrubbing a table provides the opportunity for repetitive circular movements. The seemingly simple act of scrubbing a table also provides a learning experience for a child's internal fascination with sequence and an orderly progression. The child experiences the logic of wetting and soaping the sponge, then scrubbing, rinsing, and drying the table.

In another Practical Life exercise, a two-and-a-half-year-old child sits and spoons grains from one bowl to another, over and over again. To an observing adult, this repetitive activity looks ridiculous and like a waste of time, however, a child is fascinated with fine motor activities. This exercise is the perfect match for a child.

Another child experiences the same sensation opening and closing a set of buckles, combing her hair, folding the snack napkins, or polishing a brass dish. As adults, we are grateful for the practical skills and respectful of a child's ability to develop and later apply these skills. However, for the child in a Montessori environment, these activities serve a much higher purpose—the development of the self as well as the inner capacities for muscular control and orderly thinking.

In Practical Life an older child, about age four or five, may carefully and thoughtfully arrange a bouquet of flowers and place them on a friend's worktable. This child doesn't think about the high level of coordination needed to cut through the flower stem, nor does the child think about the mathematical precision required to cut that stem right at the point where it fits perfectly into the chosen vase. The child doesn't realize that he is developing his own sense of what is aesthetically pleasing to his eye. He just knows that he likes to arrange flowers and share them as a gift for a friend. He is contributing to the life of his small community.

THE VALUE OF ANALYZED MOVEMENTS

Dr. Montessori perceived two major obstacles preventing young children from participating in the life of their community. The first of these was the lack of child-sized and child-proportioned tools to use in the activities.

The second obstacle was a child's lack of clarity regarding the specific movements needed to carry out the activities. Most

Montessori Magnet School, Hartford, CT

Folding the snack napkins is a Practical Life activity.

160

adults are models for the overt activities, but are not good models in slowing down their movements so a child can see each movement individually.

Children are driven to imitate adult activities as a way to learn these distinctly human tasks. Imitation is a sufficient motivation for beginning the activity, but children need the opportunities to carry out the movements for their own benefit and with their own personal style. A Montessori teacher models Practical Life activities with slow, analyzed movements so a child's absorbent mind can observe and assimilate the nature and the sequence of the movements that lead to a fluid whole.

Once a child has observed the teacher, then she takes over the activity, carrying out the movements as best she can on her own. It is through each child's own individualized practice that he or she builds the harmony between the brain and the muscles. Making errors in the process motivates children to spontaneously make adaptations to improve their competence with an activity.

For example, when a child first gets the Practical Life lesson for arranging flowers and then takes over the work, he often cuts the stem too short and the flower falls into the vase, or he leaves the stem too long and the flower falls out of the vase. In the process, he may have spilled the water as he poured it into the small opening of the vase, not remembering to use the small funnel designated as a help. He may only put one or two flowers into each vase with no sense of variety or personal aesthetics.

Over time, this child will refine his movements with flower arranging and become more efficient and effective, and eventually build muscular memory. All this is done via the intrinsic motivators of the unconscious mind. This child does not know or understand the powers that drive him to seek out and repeat these activities, but he does keep repeating them, building confidence and skills along the way.

With the awakening of the conscious awareness around age four, a child becomes increasingly aware of the skills he already possesses and the natural opportunities to use these skills in the surrounding life of the community. It is a delight to the child who now finds himself in the position of assisting not only himself but others around him.

The opportunity to apply new skills for oneself and for others goes far beyond arranging flowers. Children in the Montessori Children's House delight in helping one another. You will observe children helping other classmates by tying an apron, starting the zipper on a winter jacket, or pouring a glass of juice for a younger child.

Several years ago, I had a two-and-a-half-year-old girl in my class who always spilled the juice when she prepared her morning snack. Mary would faithfully retrieve the clean-up sponge and wipe up the juice on the floor as best she could, which was really not very well! By early afternoon, the juice residue would truly be a sticky mess, which provided a perfect opportunity for an older boy, Gabriel, to start his afternoon with a bit of floor scrubbing. No one suggested this activity to Gabriel nor was it his "job" according to an arbitrary jobs chart. Gabriel chose to start his afternoon doing something practical, but useful, in response to a need that he noticed. In doing this, Gabriel was no longer just a *participant* in life, but a contributor to life. Eventually, Gabriel had to find another "practical life starter" for the afternoon once Mary learned to pour successfully!

MASTERING COORDINATION

Dr. Montessori was observant that there is a time and place for children to engage in activities that focus on muscles for the express purpose of mastering coordination. Some Practical Life lessons support this idea and in time children have conscious control over their movement. The Montessori environment provides specific activities for this purpose. Two of those activities are Walking on the Line and the Silence Exercises. In these activities, the child first focuses on the mechanics of walking with natural steps. Then the child walks in a group learning to keep an even space between herself and the child in front of her. She learns when to start and when to stop in collaboration with the rest of the group, pacing herself.

Later, the child experiences walking heel-to-toe, following a prescribed line. She discovers that this takes much greater equilibrium. With practice, the child discovers that she can walk in this controlled manner without "airplane arms" for counter-balancing and when she wants a greater challenge, she can even walk along a designated line carrying objects.

A child may progress to walking on a raised line and even a balance beam several inches off the floor. Adults take these abilities for granted, and often forget that children must learn these physical movements with repeated practice.

As a child begins to master the ability to maintain stabilized equilibrium under these conditions, she is introduced to the exercises that involve changing the center of gravity by carrying objects with extended arms and eventually balancing items within an established line of gravity. The increasing degree of difficulty comes with the fact that equilibrium is gradually maintained even though the support base of the body is in constantly changing motion.

One day while observing a Montessori classroom, I witnessed a four-year-old boy determined to walk all the way around the ellipse (a line of tape on the floor) with a soft beanbag on his head. Because of the distraction of a group of friends playfully urging him on, he had great difficulty, never making it more than half-way before the beanbag would slip off. However, he was not to be deterred and fortunately, the friends got bored just watching and went on to other activities. The walker kept at it until after about fifteen minutes he succeeded. His dance of delight was spontaneous and heart-warming! Then, as if to verify that he could really do it, he started once again. After several more successful repetitions, the boy was satisfied and went off to another work choice.

Helfrich Photo Collection

Walking on the line in a Montessori classroom in Thailand.

We have all witnessed a child walking along the crack in a sidewalk or along a narrow, concrete block wall on a street. It is the same internal need to challenge one's powers of controlled movement. Not every child has the block wall or the sidewalk to inspire this challenge, so in Montessori we provide the opportunity.

The Silence Exercises challenge children to manifest control of movement by practicing their ability to not move. This requires an act of will and the mastery of the muscles with the mind. While this is virtually impossible for children under the age of about three and a half, children older than that love playing the Silence Game. In my own classrooms, children loved playing this game, and I always viewed this as a point of arrival in the development of the group of children. Over the series of exercises, the children gradually bring their muscles into a state of stillness, which allows them to develop a sense of self-control.

Dr. Montessori discovered quite by accident that children love the challenge of being still. One day, a parent came to school with a newborn baby. The children noticed how quiet the baby was even though she was very alert and taking in all that was happening. Dr. Montessori wondered out loud if the children could be as still and as quiet as the baby. Quickly, the children sat down, quieted their voices, and stopped all movement. They were able to maintain this condition for a good ten minutes.

Since then, the experiment has been repeated hundreds of thousands of times in Montessori Children's Houses worldwide. The same phenomenon happens each time. The children love to challenge themselves to be very still. In time, they begin to recognize the small, white noise sounds they can only hear when they are quiet. As a part of this exercise, they love to sit quietly and listen intently for the teacher to whisper their names to call them to gather.

An adult might observe this exercise and wonder what magic control the teacher has over the children, but there is none. The teacher invites each child to participate in the silence game. Each child chooses whether or not to join in the exercise. Those who participate want to be still and quiet, not just for their own benefit but for the success of the whole group. This sense of self-control is essential to the development of spontaneous discipline. This exercise helps a child realize that he has control over his body. He can choose when to move, how to move, and when to resist movement.

The fact that these activities have served an overtly functional purpose for the child is not the only result. Dr. Montessori realized the coordination of muscles, the harmonious carrying out of movements, and the capacity for refinement has all assisted the fuller development of a child's mind. These exercises build neurological pathways and the child prepares the foundational tools for the reasoning mind.

Movements carried out for any purpose do provide stimulation for building neural networks in the brain, especially networks between the right and the left hemispheres. However, Montessori environments intentionally and systematically help a child lay down an electrical wiring system within the walls of the brain, all in readiness for later learning. These exercises also develop a child's sense of accomplishment and a sense of personal control. The child feels strong, capable, and competent. Certainly, this is a great state of being for a six year old who will be ready to transition into the Second Plane of development.

Sensorial Exercises

Activities associated with the sensorial materials support all the sensitive periods in some manner but are geared most specifically to support the sensitive periods for order and the refinement of sensory perceptions. A child at three years old has already gathered extensive sensory data and has formed the basic classification schemata of the mind. One might think that this aspect of a child's development is complete at this point, however, this is not the case. Now, the child needs to explore all the physical aspects of the world with the conscious mind.

For example, a three-year-old child has numerous recorded experiences related to the perception of color, but these experiences have come from interacting with a variety of objects that also embody shape and dimension. A red ball is not only red, but it is also a spherical shape and has inherent weight. A red paper box is not only red, but it is a rectangular prism and because it is paper, it is light in weight. When a child plays with these objects, she perceives them as a whole entity and not the sum of the physical qualities that make up the object.

Montessori materials are called "materialized abstractions" because each set of materials represents some aspect of the physical world. By design, these materials are physical representations of an abstract quality. For instance, qualities such as "heavy" or "red" do not exist separate from the objects in which they are reflected. The notion of "red" or "heavy" are abstracts. Montessori materials are designed so that one specific quality is built into a limited set of items. This set then allows the child to explore the specific abstract quality without any other confusing or conflicting information.

For example, the abstract notion of color is isolated in a representational piece of Montessori material—the boxes of color tablets. All of the tablets are wood with the same shape and size. As a child explores the color tablets, the only information that can be used to discern similarities and differences is color. In this sensorial activity, a child actively engages with the materials, picking the tablets up, touching them, studying the various colors. By personally exploring the tablets, a child can further organize with clarity and precision her understanding of colors.

Typically, a child explores the color tablets by matching or pairing identical or related pieces. For instance, with the first two color boxes a child is looking for identical tablets that go together. If she gets to the end and the last two tablets don't match, she has a signal that she made an error somewhere along the line. No adult needs to point out the error or worry about whether it gets fixed. The child will either note the error and be challenged to resolve the mistake or she will decide it is unimportant and move on to other exercises.

Children also work with Montessori sensorial materials that involve sound cylinders, bells, smelling jars, tasting bottles, and touch tablets. All of these follow the same protocol. They isolate one particular physical quality as it exists in the world, allowing the child to explore just that one quality. The child applies the same matching of identical pieces to the exploration at hand.

Another version of pairing is found in the Geometry Cabinet where a child matches the shapes to the opening in the frame that represents that shape. This is different from the matching of identical pieces. In this case, the child matches the cut out shape with the opening of the frame that it fits neatly into. The outline of the shape within the empty frame represents the shape that fits. This activity offers a different kind of mental challenge: the child has to see the outline of the shape and the form as identical. The child uses the same approach to match a set of ten wooden cylinders into the block from which they are cut. This Montessori activity is called Cylinder Blocks.

A child who has been matching puzzle pieces into the cut-outs in a puzzle has already experienced this way of thinking. The work with the cylinder blocks, the leaf cabinet, and the geography puzzle maps all follow this same pattern. In most of these scenarios, a child knows if a mistake has been made because a piece has no place to go when they get to the end of the activity.

While matching would seem to be sufficient for a child to create classifications for all the physical qualities, it is not enough in order to create refined powers of discrimination. This requires an activity based on compare and contrast. The mind must discern the degree of similarity and the degree of difference. This is generally reflected in the activity called "grading." The third box of color tablets challenges the child to see more than just the difference between different colors, such as red and blue, but to discern differences between shades of the same color. A Montessori child would say, "Red is red, until I have seven shades of red."

Most of the Montessori materials that allow for matching also lend themselves to the activity of grading. Some materials offer matching and grading with the same items, such as sound cylinders, touch tablets, and bells. But some qualities require an additional set of materials for grading as in the case of the color

Montessori Magnet School, Hartford, CT

Classmates using the Grading Color Box 3.

tablets. The ability to grade items into a continuum allows a child to learn even more precise vocabulary.

Once a child learns the comparative and/or superlative language with one gradation, he can readily apply it to the others. For instance, a child learns what makes an object "thicker and thinner," or "thickest and thinnest." With Montessori materials, a child learns to recognize "louder and softer," and "heaviest and lightest."

After a couple of sensorial lessons, the child already knows a "dark red" color tablet, or tastes something that he identifies as "salty." But now with this ability to grade items, he discovers that he can describe "darker red" and can taste something that is the "saltiest." The child looks at a long stick and calls it longer, not yet realizing it could be the longest stick on the playground! Why is it important for a child to have this vocabulary readily at hand? This allows him a richer, more precise vocabulary for communication.

Precise vocabulary also provides a foundation for a child to draw upon when he begins to read and write around age five. When a child begins to spontaneously write, his more refined vocabulary will allow him to write a more descriptive story. Everyone appreciates an author who uses vivid descriptions to draw a picture for the reader!

ABSTRACTIONS FOR LIFE

The goal of the Montessori materials is to provide physical representations of abstractions that allow children to revisit all the previously recorded sensory data since they were infants, and now build usable abstractions for life. The capacity for conscious memory is attached to the abstraction—knowledge that exists in the brain without the need for external stimuli. Building memory is important and becomes accessible with the connection to language. The connection with the precise language also serves to fix the abstraction in a child's mind.

A child knows what he knows once it can be named. For example, a child who recognizes the rectangular piece from the

Geometry Cabinet soon begins to see rectangles in the windows, the door, the lids of boxes, and the rug he puts under his work. The child delights in being able to name these shapes—square, rectangle, triangle, hexagon, quatrefoil—taking for granted that everyone knows what he is talking about.

Children love to learn new words and they enjoy the opportunity to use them. I remember a four-year-old boy who had just learned the names of several land and water forms. Before I knew it, he was at the world globe finding lakes, islands, gulfs, and archipelagos. Having this precise language allowed this boy to use his knowledge to stimulate other kinds of discoveries.

Once a child has explored all the individual sensory qualities, he is able to connect this experience back to the real world. A child is able to use this knowledge to recognize these same qualities as they are spontaneously manifested in the surrounding world. For instance, at this point a Montessori teacher will introduce the child to materials for further exploration that prepare the child's mind for later studies in algebra, geometry and geography. Certainly, the four year old is unaware that the Trinomial Cube is anything more than an interesting three-dimensional puzzle. It will be years later that this child makes the connection to the algebraic formula $(a+b+c)^3$. In the same manner, the child has no idea that his work with the constructive triangles in the Montessori Children's House provides an experiential foundation for the study of geometric theorems.

These two examples reflect a basic Montessori principle of "indirect preparation," which means early childhood explorations that are sensory-based prepare a child's mind by seeding the field for later abstract studies. A couple years later, the child will meet these concepts again in the abstract form with his reasoning mind in the Second or Third Planes of development. At this point, the young person recognizes his familiarity with a topic as he taps into unconscious knowledge already in place in a concrete experiential form.

PREPARATION FOR HANDWRITING

Another manifestation of indirect preparation inherent in Montessori work with the sensorial materials is the preparation of the hand for writing. As a young child traces her fingers around the figures of the geometry cabinet, her mind is focused on the differences in shapes. At the same time, she is subconsciously training her hand muscles to follow a defined contour. This is important for a young child between two and three-and-a-half years old because this is when her tactile sensitivity is the highest. It is also at this time when a child derives the greatest brain stimulation from tactile stimulation.

In Montessori, the teacher offers a child a set of rough and smooth boards with alternating sections of light sandpaper and smooth painted wood. The work with the rough/smooth boards and tablets focuses on tactile discrimination of differences in texture, but indirectly allows the hand to develop a delicate lightness of touch when the mind is ready for writing. Sometime later, a child's hand will have built into its muscular memory the basic tools needed to carry out the art of handwriting.

LANGUAGE

At age three, a child typically has already learned to speak, has a small vocabulary of several hundred words, and has intuited the whole structure of the grammar and syntax of his native language. Now, the child becomes a voracious "vocabulary caterpillar," gobbling up all the vocabulary associated with the growing world of life experiences. The child is validating knowledge and increasing his powers of communication.

For some children, they are still mastering pronunciation of certain letter sounds or words. All children need opportunities to explore modes of verbal communication. Unfortunately, many children have not had a strong experience of being listened to by adults or in learning how to shape thoughts into clear articulations.

Montessori activities begin with an extensive component of spoken language activities. For example, a Montessori teacher will engage a child in a conversation around an interesting picture on the wall, which ultimately is demonstrating to the child how to carry on a conversation with another person. A Montessori teacher also tells the children in her class true stories about everyday life experiences, such as waiting for the gatekeeper to unlock the gate on the way to work, or a trip to the post office. Or she might bring cultural objects or photos of famous people to the class and tell true stories about these people or items. By doing this, the teacher is demonstrating to the children how to share and tell stories. In time, the teacher will ask the students to bring items to share and tell stories about.

These are simple activities that parents can engage in as well. Spontaneous conversations are just that—spontaneous moments when a parent and a child can talk together about something they are interested in or random moments when a parent can share interesting information about something the child has discovered. These simple activities form the foundation for later explorations in writing and reading; explorations that are also begun in the Children's House.

Montessori teachers support families by helping them understand their children's early language development and encourage adults to speak with their children—not just at them but with them! It is important for families to provide a rich linguistic environment for their children. This complements Montessori activities.

All the language activities associated with Montessori's Oral Language and Enrichment of Vocabulary materials are critical tools for meeting a child's language needs. These activities begin on the day children arrive in the Children's House. Often, these spoken language activities are "hidden" because there are few tangible materials on the shelves to remind Montessori teachers to do them daily. It takes a diligent and prepared Montessori teacher to remember to carry out these kinds of spoken language activities with the children on a daily basis.

In addition to "Telling True Stories" and spontaneous conversations, other simple exercises consist of reading a variety of good literature, including poetry. Montessori teachers also provide opportunities for vocabulary related to sets of interesting picture cards, and the formal activity called the "Question Game," which involves asking a series of questions about an experience or event that a small group of children have participated in.

One day, just as I arrived to visit a school, the fire alarm sounded for the regular once-a-month fire drill. After the children returned to their classroom, the Montessori student/ teacher engaged the group in the question game. She asked: "What happened?" "Who was involved?" "Where did you go?" "How long were you outside?" "Why did you have a fire drill?"

The Question Game helps a child discover that these same questions are useful in composing a story, whether it is a verbal story about an object she has brought to school to share with her classmates, or a story she is writing about something she experienced. These language activities allow the child to hear, see, and experience language in its natural context.

The teacher telling true stories becomes the catalyst for the child to tell his/her own true story. The ability to compose a story verbally becomes the precursor to the ability to compose a written story. True stories don't have to be long or exotic, they just need to be factual and interesting, and they certainly don't have to always be about the parent or the teacher.

Every single card in a set of classified cards on the Montessori language shelf or a picture in a book should be worthy of one true story. I had one particular card in the United States' history card set that the older children just loved. It was a simple drawing of the famous Native American woman, Sacajawea, who was a guide and interpreter for the famous explorers, Lewis and Clark, who led an expedition to the Western United States in 1804. In the drawing, the three of them are standing on a bluff looking off into the distance. For a month or so, the children would bring this card to me and ask for another story about Sacajawea. Each story would tell one more little bit about the interesting adventures of Sacajawea and Lewis and Clark as they traversed across wild and unexplored territory to the Pacific Ocean at the beginning of the 1800s.

In another history card set, one particular boy loved the pictures of the U.S. presidents. It wasn't enough for Nathan to just know the names of the presidents; he wanted to know about the individual men. So each time he brought a picture card, I would share one more little bit of information. " Grover Cleveland was president two different times. William Taft weighed over 300 pounds. William Henry Harrison caught pneumonia at his inauguration because he refused to wear his overcoat. He died shortly after. Theodore Roosevelt and Franklin Roosevelt were cousins. John Adams was the father of John Quincy Adams. Dolly Madison commissioned John Phillips Sousa to compose 'Hail to the Chief' because her husband, James Madison was so short that no one noticed when he entered the room. The music, "Hail to the Chief," was used to announce President Madison's arrival and it has been used ever since to signal the arrival of a president."

Nathan loved hearing all these interesting details about U.S. presidents because it made them more human and memorable. If we think about history's lively details and the famous yet very human people who are keys to history, we would never run out of inspiration for true stories. A parent or teacher might have to do a little research, but remember, you are telling this story to three-to-six-year-old children. They are interested in the most basic information and will be interested if you are.

VOCABULARY RICH MONTESSORI ENVIRONMENTS

The Montessori exercises developed for Enrichment of Vocabulary feed a child's insatiable appetite for new vocabulary. For the new students in the Children's House, the teacher begins simply by giving the names of all the exercises in the Montessori

classroom as well as the names of all the objects that exist within this prepared environment. The child learns the name of the exercises that are being presented to her, "spooning, table washing, buttons frame." The child also learns the names of the objects that she uses to carry out these activities. For example, in shoe polishing the child learns vocabulary words related to the activity, such as applicator brush, shining brush, buffer, polish tin, and the newspaper underlay.

The sensorial materials themselves allow for the expansion of vocabulary, especially adjectives associated with the qualities that the materials represent. For example, the sound cylinders can teach the difference between loud and soft; the baric tables can show what is heavy and what is light; and pieces of cloth demonstrate the textures of silk, wool, and cotton. The language of "thick and thin" can be associated with a set of brown wooden prisms. The vocabulary for shapes can be attached to the pieces inside the geometry cabinet or the set of geometric solids; rectangle, right-angled scalene triangle, pentagon, parallelogram, rectangular prism, and cylinder, just for starters!

Sets of picture cards organized by specific classifications further expand a child's word horizons. These exercises integrate scientific and cultural subjects as the child learns the names of the various continents and countries of the world, the names of animals representing all the phyla of the animal kingdom, and the names of indigenous plants and flowers, among many other topics. What four year old is not fascinated by the world of dinosaurs? Children are fascinated by dinosaur pictures and love to wrap their tongues around the complex names for brontosaurus, stegosaurus, or pterodactyl.

In the Montessori classroom, the teacher offers children cards representing famous composers, famous artists, or scientists, and the creations and tools that they use. Children discover famous places in the world and different ways that humans have met their basic needs throughout their history. The possibilities for expanding vocabulary are endless in the Montessori environment.

EXERCISES TO INCREASE VOCABULARY

Parents often wonder how a teacher can help a child learn so much vocabulary in such a short period of time. Just responding to a child's query, "What's that?" would not be sufficient. A Montessori teacher uses a marvellous technique that Dr. Montessori discovered in the writings of Dr. Eduard Séguin called the "Three Period Lesson."

It is a simple lesson that can be used with any child over the age of two-and-a-half years. Parents can use this technique as readily as a Montessori teacher. You can use a simplified version of this technique with even younger children. The child typically chooses three variables (pictures or objects) at a time. Let's use the example of naming vegetable cards from a simple set of pictures. The first part of the lesson consists of pointing to the item and naming it. "This is a carrot." "This is an asparagus." "This is a cabbage." While the teacher names the object, she/he points to the picture card. Most adults would think this exercise seems too simple, and would want to add questions about the description or share additional information about the objects. Dr. Montessori agreed with what Dr. Séguin had already discovered—an excess of words confuses a child. The same is true today. By the time an adult gets through the explanation, the child has completely forgotten the name of the object that he was supposed to remember. So we keep it simple. This allows for a child to learn a word and retain it.

The second part of the lesson is where the real learning happens. It is in this context that a child builds a clear neural pathway in the brain connecting an image and its name. We already know that the building of a usable neural pathway requires repetition of the related information so that the synaptic connections become strong and solid. So, in this part of the lesson, we play a game. The adult gives a simple command using the new vocabulary. We might say, "Put your hand above the cabbage. Touch the asparagus. Place the carrot here." By responding to the request, the child engages both her mind and her body in the building of the connection.

An experienced parent or teacher will have a series of ten to fifteen commands that can be used in a quick delivery, which becomes part of the fun of the game, as well as a way to build neural pathways for learning vocabulary. This allows a child to become fully engaged and gives him or her time to sort out any initial confusion with the three names. The number of picture cards can always be decreased to two if needed so a child can be successful at the game. Once in awhile, a child doesn't get the confusion sorted out. This usually reflects a lack of sufficient experience with the object or classification of objects upon which to attach the language. In this instance, we make a "graceful end" by simply repeating the information given in the first part of the lesson, which involves naming each item.

Most of the time a child gets quite confident and consistent in responding to the commands, indicating that the connections are crystallizing. At this point, we do the third part of the lesson, which is simply a moment of verification. We point to each individual picture and ask, "What's this?" The child is now challenged to bring forth the name using his own memory.

If you do this with your child, don't be surprised or dismayed when he or she only remembers some of the items the next day. This is knowledge "under construction" and the final nails are still not in place, but the forms are there! A few more repetitions in a playful manner, without recriminations, will serve to solidify the new vocabulary. Once the new names are fixed in your child's mind, you will be amazed to hear your child use this vocabulary as comfortably as if he or she had always known it. The new vocabulary becomes part of their everyday, usable language.

There are so many options in the Montessori language area in the Children's House that a child can never fully tap all the materials, even over a three-year time period. A Montessori teacher does not have a checklist of what must be covered, but she must continue to offer variety and depth to whatever interests each child spontaneously brings to the classroom or to whatever interests stimulate the teacher. This approach allows each child to move ahead at his or her own pace, or take additional time if needed. Just as all children do not learn to walk or talk at the same time, children also learn the names of different things at different paces, depending on their particular interests.

All the richness reflected in the Montessori materials for spoken language creates a foundation for later explorations in reading. In addition, vocabulary the child learns from his parents adds further richness and diversity to this whole experience.

LEARNING TO READ IN MONTESSORI

A child meets familiar vocabulary as he begins to learn to read. Knowing the names of the pictures already offers a child a greater interest and chance of success in reading. The same picture cards that a child used for expanding his vocabulary now reappear along with labels that can be matched to the pictures.

A child discovers he can sound out some of the familiar names and then uses the context of the classification as a clue to reading the labels that are more challenging. For instance, a child might be reading the labels for things you see in the kitchen. He can read "cabinet, bowl, sink, or oven" by just sounding out the label. When he gets to more challenging words such as "refrigerator or teaspoon," he sounds out what he can and then looks at the pictures that are missing labels to see if he can figure out which one it goes to. This actually allows a child to read many labels that would be beyond his skill level if there were no picture to match it to.

Montessori teachers call this set of activities "Reading Classification," which is a large section of the language area. Montessori teachers organize sets of cards by classifications, offering a child a systematic view of how the world is organized. Sets of pictures can range from simple common groupings such as "Things Along the Street," "Different Modes of Transportation," or "Articles of Clothing," to more complex sets that represent classifications of art, music, history, geography, botany, zoology, and physical science. Some examples of more complex sets include "Impressionist Paintings," "Instruments of the Orchestra," "Presidents of the USA," "Famous Places in the World," "Insects," "Plants of Australia," or "Instruments in a Science Laboratory."

The sets of cards for Reading Classification can be used in different ways, creating greater challenges as the child advances. They consist of picture cards, labels to match with the pictures, and an additional set of the same picture cards with the labels still attached that are called the "control cards." These kinds of reading exercises allow a child to work independently. A child can check her own work with the set of matching control cards. She can match the pictures and read the labels to see if they are the same. There is no shame in making a mistake and no intimidation with someone else pointing out the student's mistakes. If her answers are wrong, she simply switches the mismatched labels. With these Montessori materials, a child builds confidence in reading and practices with cards that interest her, which stimulates even more practice.

In a Montessori classroom, there are simple books with interesting but skill appropriate text for a child to read. Parents often hear that Montessori teachers don't use books for children to read. What is accurate is that teachers do not typically use a programmed reading series that adults might remember from their own school days. In a Montessori environment, there is no regimented reading program where a child must first read Book One, followed by Book Two. Montessori teachers have a variety of interesting simple books for a child to choose from. Children are free to choose any one of a variety of books to read according to individual interests. Sometimes, a child does take a book that has words she can't read, but most often she just asks an older child for some help, or she chooses to read just the words she knows.

LEARNING GRAMMAR AND SYNTACTICAL ORDER

As a child becomes a more confident reader, there are additional reading exercises in the Children's House that allow a child to explore the power of words and how they can be organized grammatically or syntactically. These simple reading exercises serve to enrich the child's own written creations as they discover the world of adjectives and adverbs, and the kinds of information you can put into a sentence.

For instance, a child reads short phrases on slips of paper that might say "the brown horse," or "the silly goose," or "the mother pig." The teacher offers a colored symbol to attach to words that are nouns, a different colored symbol for words that are adjectives, and a third colored symbol to identify the articles "a" and "the." The child cuts the slip of paper and plays with the order of the words to see that in English the phrase only makes sense when the adjective is between the article and the noun. The same basic symbols can be used for almost any written language as every language consists of nouns, verbs, adjectives, and conjunctions. The placement order of the symbols will change according to the syntactical order of the particular language. For example, in German the verb is most often at the end of the sentence or phrase. In the Thai language, the adjective always follows the noun.

An advanced set of exercises introduces the concept of a noun being a subject or an object in a sentence. In a simple sentence, such as "Thomas throws the ball," the subject, "Thomas," cannot be interchanged with the direct object, "ball." When the child reads, "the ball throws Thomas," he laughs at the silliness and needs no explanation to know that this syntactical order makes no sense!

My best advice to parents is to resist the temptation to teach your child to read and write. Trust your child's Montessori teacher and let the process happen spontaneously. What you can do is support the child's interest in writing and reading. Let him write pieces to the best of his ability. Don't worry if the writing is not very legible in the beginning or if your child can't read every slip of paper he brings home to share. Keep encouraging his or her interest in writing, and do not worry about spelling, legibility, and organization. Those skills will come later!

It is also important to recognize that many Montessori schools begin with a cursive font instead of print as it follows more naturally the movements of a child's hand. Also, Montessori children learn the sounds of the letters before they match these sounds to the names of the letters. They use this approach because it is the sounds of the letters that facilitate reading, not the names. Parents can support their children by reinforcing these two approaches, and if they are engaging their children, be consistent in using these protocols.

As a child progresses to reading phrases, sentences, and eventually simple books, he rediscovers books and information that he has already heard read to him and loves.

Montessori Approach to Math

Early support for the mathematical mind in Montessori activities has prepared children for work in arithmetic. They already have had extensive experience with patterns and sequential progressions. This orientation toward life can now be applied in the science of mathematics.

In Montessori, a child begins with a basic orientation to numbers (quantities and symbols) for 1 to 10. Montessori activities with the materials build upon the capacity to recognize one-to-one correspondence as well as the spontaneous use of number names in the real world. A child applies one-to-one correspondence as she counts the sections on a number rod and applies the language she has heard before—one, two, three, four, etc.

A child has who counted all kinds of items spontaneously recognizes the vocabulary used in counting. At around four years old, a child is ready to apply this vocabulary to the formal counting of sets of objects. In the past, many educators believed that a child was unable to comprehend mathematical principles until about age six. This belief was based on approaches that required a young child to deal with quantities as a set of individual items together. Dr. Montessori observed that a child sees two sticks as one and one—not two. She realized that the separateness of the objects was an obstacle for the young child. She looked at the red rods used to represent different lengths in the sensorial area and realized that she could use something similar to introduce a young child (about age four) to the notion of quantity in a new way.

Dr. Montessori created the number rods, which are rods painted in two colors in alternating sections to represent the series of quantities from one to ten in increasing ten centimetre lengths. The key difference is that the rod representing "3" is a single rod not three separate rods. The relationship of this "3-rod" to the longer "4-rod" and the shorter "2-rod" will always be the same. The difference is always the same length—ten centimeters more or ten centimeters less.

The child who uses the Montessori rods as the first way to experience quantity gets less confused because she can count alternating red and blue sections accurately. With the red and blue number rods as the key, Dr. Montessori discovered that even a young child could understand quantity. She also realized that a child could quickly make a transition to quantity as separate objects without any confusion. Very soon, the child sees how to count a set of wooden spindles into a box with numbered compartments.

In her first Children's Houses, Dr. Montessori had an astounding discovery—if the young children could count to ten, they were ready for an introduction to the decimal system! This was difficult for Dr. Montessori to believe at first, but repeatedly the children demonstrated to her that not only were they interested in the decimal system materials, but they could really understand the inherent concepts through sensorial experience. Since the decimal system is a system of counting based on the powers of ten, Dr. Montessori designed a set of materials starting with the individual unit as the base. This physical representation of the hierarchies of the decimal system made it easy for young children to grasp the pieces literally and the concepts mentally!

The four-year-old children in Dr. Montessori's Children's Houses were fascinated by the beautiful sets of golden beads initially designed for the older elementary age children. The concrete nature of these beads allows a child to experience tactilely the mathematical concepts that have traditionally only been presented in an abstract form. With the Montessori golden beads, the youngsters in the Children's House can actually hold and feel a bar of 10 beads, or a square with 100 beads, or a cube with 1000 beads.

The children learn the names for units, tens, hundreds, and thousands as easily as they learn the names of different fruits or dinosaurs. A young child can quickly grasp the idea of counting to ten and then it becomes the next piece, which is the dynamic nature of the decimal system. Now, the child can see how ten unit beads strung together make a 10 bar, ten of these 10 bars strung together make a 100 square, and ten of the hundreds stacked together make a 1000 cube.

With this basic understanding and the ability to recognize and read up to four-digit composite numbers, such as 1396, a Montessori teacher can now introduce a child to the four mathematical operations— addition, subtraction, multiplication and division. While this might seem a stretch for a young child, Dr. Montessori discovered that children as young as four can understand basic mathematical concepts when they are presented in a concrete, tactile, experiential form long before moving to the symbolic abstract representations.

A child actually carries out the "drama" called addition to build understanding of the nature of the operation before he ever sees an addition equation in a written form. I call this activity a "drama" because in a Montessori environment, a child actually experiences the process of addition with her whole body. She made the addition happen together with her two friends who poured their beads together with hers to get the final result.

Current research in child development verifies this physical approach to mathematics, something Dr. Montessori understood nearly a hundred years ago. Once again, the abstract concept built upon the physical sensory experiences of the child, are much stronger and more usable concepts. Even when a child begins to use written equations, she still uses stamps, dots, beads or wooden strips to support the concrete experience as a companion to the work with the written equations.

TRANSITIONING TO THE ABSTRACT

As the human tendency for exactness and precision becomes more important in the life of the older child, five to six years old, children want to be free of the concrete materials. They have a strong desire to simplify all processes and this provides the motivation for mastery of the basic memorized facts for each mathematical operation, such as the addition tables, the subtraction tables, and the times table.

A boy learning addition using the Strip Board.

Montessori Magnet School, Hartford, CT

In the Montessori classroom, a child uses concrete materials and meets these simple equations in a variety of novel pathways that lead spontaneously to memorization through repetition. For example, a child discovers the basic combinations for addition by playing the Snake Game, which is a series of colored bead bars ranging from one to nine in value. The child makes a serpentine snake with these bead bars and then by counting sets of ten, he converts the snake into a series of golden ten-bars. The child spontaneously experiences that 3 and 5 makes an 8, or that a 10 and a 5 makes a 15. The child sees this combination as represented by a ten-bar and a five-bar since the snake is based on sets of tens, but the child recognizes the result of these two bars are 15 from his work with teens where the quantity was created with the same sets of bead-bars.

Shortly thereafter, a child discovers the same combinations through her work with the Addition Strip Board, which is a board with rows and columns of squares. The child uses a set of blue strips ranging in value from one to nine, and a set of red strips with the same values. The child places a blue strip and a red strip end to end and reads the combined result in the numbers at the top of the board. With this material, the child can also discover all the ways to make a sum of twelve, as well as the fact that 3 + 9 is the same as 9 + 3. The teacher does not necessarily tell the child that this is "the nature of the commutative law," but the child has experienced this basic mathematical law. One day, the child will be able to define the commutative law; when you add or multiply numbers, the order doesn't matter.

The memorization of the addition combinations is reinforced once again with the four different kinds of addition finger charts, which are basic matrix boards with the values one to nine across the top and down the left side. By using a series of simple finger movements, a child works out addition combinations and finds the answer in the numbers filling the rest of the board. In each of these contexts, a child sees 7 + 8 = 15, over and over again.

She builds the equation in a concrete way with beads or strips, and then finds the same equation on each of the finger charts. After awhile, she realizes that this is a constant, and the partial equation of 7 + 8 will always equal 15! The child has opportunities to write the equation in its totality as well, filling in answers in booklets or writing equations as a whole. Each repetition helps a child to eventually hold this significant piece of information in her memory, ready for whenever it is needed.

Again, each child's approach to learning arithmetic is so different from that of most adults. If we were to sit and go through all the addition equations with a friend, we would tend to be discouraged by how many we still have to work on. Most children do not see learning as a discouraging process but rather as a joyful one.

Not long ago, I watched two children going through a complete set of the addition combinations—all 81! When the first boy got to the end, he asked the girl to count how many were in the "unknown" pile. He crowed with delight when the number was only ten! He wasn't deflated because he had gotten ten wrong. Instead, he was delighted to only have ten more to focus on! What a wonderful lesson for an adult to see how to perceive the glass as "half full"—or better yet, as completely full! The other child then took her turn and was at an earlier addition skill level. She was not embarrassed or intimidated by her growing pile of unknowns, but instead continued to work. In addition, the other student she was working with kept encouraging her. Interestingly, the children did not keep count on who was further ahead! As I observed this interaction, I thought, What a great way to honor her desire and respect her dignity! No adult or teacher told these two classmates how to handle this situation; they spontaneously manifested this shared learning experience.

MONTESSORI TEACHERS AND MATERIALS

Montessori teachers are engaged in important work. Fortunately, these teachers have great tools to assist them. By their design, Montessori materials can take children to greater heights and help them obtain solid conquests in learning. Montessori teachers also have effective techniques and activities to accompany these materials, leading a child to a rich and varied educational experience.

Add to this equation, parents who care deeply about their children's welfare and their joy of learning. Parents, always remember you are role models for your children! You are a dynamic aspect of your children's world! No one has to be perfect in this process; we just have to be diligent in offering our best to children. In this way, we all support our children in their cosmic task—the great process of self-construction!

CHAPTER TWELVE

The Future and Its Rewards

There is no doubt that parenting is a daunting task. Parents worldwide want the best for their children. But often, parents have ongoing questions about what is best in any given situation. Parents can be plagued by societal pressures or the push to make sure that their child is more successful in life than they were. Some common questions parents ask themselves during the course of raising their child:

- "What is the best for our child?"
- "Do we focus on skills and abilities, or is knowledge the most important?"
- "Do we want our child to get into the school that is the most prestigious or has the best reputation? Or do we want our child to be happy and express to us what he or she thinks is the best path?
- "Can one school fill our expectations and allow our child to find himself?
- "Is it okay for our child to make choices that do not lead to a high-paced career track or a choice that will not necessarily lead to high income brackets when he or she is an adult?"
- "When do we step in as parents to direct our children's future and when do we step out?"
- "What are our responsibilities as a parents and what are the responsibilities of the school and the teacher?"

As parents, we all know these soul-searching questions are endless. Dr. Montessori believed that the best for each child was to give him or her the opportunity to work out his or her own development to the fullest. She believed this approach would ultimately ensure that the child becomes a fully realized person. Dr. Montessori encouraged supporting a "self-directed child" rather than one who primarily took direction from others. In the end, she believed, *Yes, the child would have skills, knowledge, and abilities. He would also be a person with good character and a good sense of himself.*

Children who are supported toward the optimal fulfilment of their natural development feel differently about their experiences in life. These children develop skills and attitudes that impact not only who they are but how they think about themselves and their roles and responsibilities as members of humanity. Self-directed children grow and develop in harmony with the natural plan of life. This approach allows children to develop into self-actualized, stable, happy adults who contribute to their families, community, and perhaps the world while holding on to a clear sense of the beauty of the world and the gift of life itself. These children also have developed their spiritual sensibilities, and have a steady internal moral compass.

A Fully Developed Young Adult

Dr. Montessori believed that a child needs the whole of the Four Planes of development—all the way to age twenty-four years—to become a fully actualized human being. For some children in today's complex world, it may even take a few extra years for them to arrive at this point. But don't despair; it is possible to begin to see the essential elements growing long before your child reaches age twenty-four.

A child who experiences success in her personally chosen activities experiences self-satisfaction, joy, and delight in being successful on her own. This is stressed in Montessori education from the Children's House on up. Dr. Montessori stressed the importance of "child led" activities that encourage a child's self-motivation, natural curiosity, and wonder for learning. Dr. Montessori recognized early on that children are naturally curious and have an innate desire to learn, but what they want to learn at any one moment in time can be quite different from what another child is interested in. Giving a child freedom to choose from a variety of challenging activities allows that child to answer her own curiosity, which in turn sparks her motivation to continue to learn throughout her life just for the joy of learning

So, what does a fully developed person look like? In general, this person has few needs for protective defenses to make life tolerable. For example, since childhood this person has learned life skills that allow for independence. By the time a fully developed child becomes a young adult, he feels capable, competent, and confident. He is not afraid of new challenges and takes each new challenge as a delight. This person feels that there is nothing that can't be accomplished given the right tools and a bit of perseverance. The challenge and discovery process take on greater import than any resulting product. In essence, the journey is far more important than the destination.

The fully developed person has no need for competition. While games, rules, and team activities become important components in a child's Second Plane of development (ages six years through twelve years,) this child still carries a sense that the social interactions with others are just as important as the game. This makes it possible for your child to play a sport and enjoy the game whether her team wins or loses the game. This child is not consumed with a competitive nature and angry at herself and others if she doesn't do well. Instead, she is free to celebrate the accomplishments of others, even if those accomplishments are far beyond her own skills.

In the same vein, a fully developed young adult celebrates the accomplishments of others without diminishing her own sense of competency. This is a skill that many children and adults have difficulty developing—a skill that moves past jealousy or constantly comparing one's own talents with others. This capacity will also allow your child to freely express a sense of empathy and compassion toward others, even for competitors on an opposing team.

NO NEED FOR PERFECTION

By the time a fully developed child has become an adult, he has experienced the powerful emotions that come from meeting a challenge and successfully working it through to the end. Without any expectation of perfection, this young adult finds a level of competency that is satisfying and appropriate.

The importance of the process in obtaining knowledge and learning about the world is essential in Montessori education. This begins in the Children's House, and as a child's skill levels increase, he naturally seeks a greater level of competency. A great example is that of the young child in the Children's House just learning about the mathematical process of addition. This child is significantly challenged to just understand the nature of addition as the mathematical operation of putting quantities together to make more. It is only later that the child is confident enough in understanding the mathematical process to be interested in whether he got the right answer! There is a certain luxury, or rather, freedom to explore the dynamics of addition if the child does not have worry about getting the right answer.

If getting the right answer is necessary from the beginning, the child will seek out shortcuts to assure getting the right answer. This shortcut will also shortcut his desire to fully understand the process. It is as if the mind says, "Why do I have to understand what I am doing, if I can just get the right answer this way?" In Montessori education, the child enjoys exploring the process. As he makes significant discoveries on his own, he builds a sense of confidence with the process, which is far more important than just getting the right answer! Once the child has a solid understanding, he exhibits a spontaneous curiosity about whether he is getting the right answer.

LOVING AND CARING FOR ONESELF AND OTHERS

The Montessori approach also encourages compassion toward others. On one occasion, I visited a classroom where one of my student teachers was practice teaching. It was the day before the winter holiday vacation and the children were doing their best to stay focused on their work. One older girl, about five years old, had a hard time choosing work and applying herself, which I determined was not meeting her teacher's expectations. My agitation with the girl must have been more obvious than I thought because before long two of the girl's friends approached me. They both said I should just ignore their friend because she was usually not like this, but she was going to visit her grandma in Florida the next day and she was really excited.

It was a humbling lesson in compassion for me, but also a wonderful example of complete understanding and compassion on the part of the girl's two friends. Earlier that day in the classroom, I had observed these same two girls as the "victims" of their friend's excitement throughout the morning. Yet, they were just letting this all roll off their backs as no big deal.

It is this kind of compassion toward others that allows a child to feel as if she is a member of a cohesive society where people accept one another's idiosyncrasies and have empathy for individual situations and capacities. Loving, caring, and concern for one's classmates become natural extensions of this compassion—a sensitivity that will last a lifetime.

Another time, I enjoyed observing loving and caring behaviour among Montessori children when my eight-year-old son played indoor soccer. The children were playing a rough and tumble game in a confined space and several children got hit full force by a kicked soccer ball. When a player on my son's team got hurt, all the teammates gathered around in an almost protective posture. Expressions of empathy came naturally and spontaneously from each. It seemed as if the injured player began feeling better immediately just having his pain acknowledged. As the game went on, the players on my son's team became as protective of the other team's players as they were of their own teammates. It was almost as if they sensed that the player—regardless of whose team he was on—needed this compassion and they were there to provide it. I don't remember who won or lost the game, but I will never forget watching these young children caring for each other.

RESPONSIBLE AND ORGANIZED

The fully developed child develops the capacity to manage his own time and sequence of activities. In the Montessori classroom, this is manifested by a child who arrives in the morning already knowing what activity to work on at the start of the day. Beginning in Children's House and continuing through Lower and Upper Elementary, Montessori teachers work with children to plan out a good part of their day or week with activities they choose to work on. This approach teaches children how to plan activities, understand time management, work independently, and follow their natural curiosity. This approach also builds responsibility. In addition, the Montessori environment supports the independent child to help others in need of assistance, and delight in sharing what he has learned with others. I have witnessed many times the older child who lovingly ties the apron strings again for a younger child, or the rush of children of all ages to help pick up the dish of beans that a very young child has spilled.

If a child is treated respectfully and as an intelligent being deserving of respect and care from the beginning, this child will most likely behave responsibly because it is the *right thing to do,* not because someone in authority is watching. Dr. Montessori understood that the way children are treated is the way they will treat others. Fear is not a healthy motivator for "good behaviour."

The desire to do the right thing for oneself and for others needs to come from within the child through her own experience. A young child (under age six years) learns to use the basic courtesies as a means to getting along with her classmates. The child between the ages of six and twelve years learns to create rules for the group. When a child is engaged in creating the rules, that child will be willing to follow those same rules. As the child becomes an adolescent, the practice of both common courtesy and an acceptance of the value of rules will allow for the building of secure, lasting, and safe personal relationships. When a child develops his own inner moral compass, it will last him a lifetime

THE ULTIMATE GIFT

Hopefully, parents can take the time and care to invest in their child from the beginning, seeing him or her from day one as an intelligent, whole person deserving of love, respect, and attention. This is the approach Montessori education engenders in its philosophy and approach to educating a child. If parents can support and encourage their child to reach for his or her fullest development as a human being, this is the ultimate gift. In turn, parents will reap the reward of one day witnessing their child as an adult with his or her own life and path, participating in the furthering of humanity.

Dr. Montessori firmly believed that the child who experienced life in this manner during the formative years would seek out similar experiences later in life. She believed that the child who grows and sees him/herself as a productive member of a positive society would grow into an adult who would desire a world that allows for similar experiences.

This is the hope for the future. This is the basis for a world society of peace and tranquillity. This is the start of a global society based upon an inherent respect for all others, recognizing the commonalities of our humanity and the richness of our differences.

ENDNOTES

CHAPTER TWO
The Relevance of Montessori in Modern Times

1. Shore, Rima. *Rethinking the Brain: New Insights into Early Development.* New York: Families and Work Institute, 1997.
2. Ibid. p.18.
3. Ibid. p.15.
4. Montessori, Maria, MD. *Spontaneous Activity in Education.* New York: Schocken Books, 1969.198.
5. Montessori, Maria, MD. *The Absorbent Mind.* New York: Delta Books, 1967. 24.
6. Shore, Rima, opt. cit. p.18.
7. Ibid. p.18.
8. Greenfield, Susan A. *BBC Brain Story: Unlocking Our Inner World of Emotions, Memories, Ideas and Desires.* London: BBC Worldwide Limited, 2000. 34, 54.
9. Montessori, Maria, MD. *Formation of Man.* Oxford, England: Clio Press, 1989. 91.
10. Montessori, Maria, MD. *The Absorbent Mind.* New York: Delta Books, 1967. 25.
11. Shore, Rima, opt.cit. p. 28.
12. Pearce, Joseph Chilton. *The Biology of Transcendence: A Blueprint of the Human Spirit.* Rochester, VT: Park Street Press, 2002. 134.
13. Erikson, Erik H. *Childhood and Society.* New York: W.W. Norton &Company, Inc.1963.
14. Shore, Rima, opt.cit. p.18.
15. Ibid. p. 39.
16. Behen, Michael E., PhD; Emily Helder, MA; Robert Rothermel, PhD; Katherine Solomon, PhD; and Harry Chugani, MD. "Incidence of Specific Absolute Neurocognitive Impairment in Globally Intact Children with Histories of Early Severe Deprivation," *Child Neuropsychology.* 2008 September: 14 (5): 453-469.
17. Montessori, Maria, MD. *The Secret of Childhood.* Notre Dame, Indiana: Fides Publishers, Inc., 1970. 39.
18. Shore, Rima, opt.cit. p.18.
19. Ibid. p. 37.
20. Restak, Richard M. *Brainscapes: An Introduction to What Neuroscience Has Learned About the Structure, Function, and Abilities of the Brain.* New York: Discover Books, 1996.
21. Montessori, Maria, MD. *The Secret of Childhood.* Notre Dame, Indiana: Fides Publishers, Inc., 1970. 38.
22. Shore, Rima, opt.cit. p. 18.
23. Montessori, Maria, MD. *The Absorbent Mind.* New York: Delta Books, 1967. 81.

CHAPTER THREE
The Big Picture of Child Development

1. Montessori, Maria, MD. "The Need for Universal Accord So That Man May Be Morally Trained to Defend Humanity." *AMI Communications,* N. 4, 2001.7.

CHAPTER FOUR
The Child's Mind

1. Montessori, Maria, MD. *Spontaneous Activity in Education.* New York: Schocken Books, 1969.198.
2. Ibid. p. 198.
3. Ibid. p. 199.
4. Ibid. p. 202.
5. Ibid. p. 205.
6. Bronowski, Jacob, PhD. *The Origins of Knowledge and Imagination.* New Haven, CT: Yale University Press, 1978. 21-22.
7. Greenfield, Susan. *BBC Brain Story.* London: BBC Worldwide Limited, 2000. 49.
8. Standing, E.M. *Maria Montessori: Her Life and Work.* New York: Penguin Putnam, Inc. (Plume), 1984. 208.
9. Greenfield, Susan. *BBC Brain Story.* London: BBC Worldwide Limited, 2000. 55.
10. Brown, Stuart, MD. "Play." *New York Times*, Feb. 17, 2008: 5.
11. Pearce, Joseph Chilton. *The Biology of Transcendence.* Rochester, VT: Park Street Press, 2002. 42.
12. Begley, Sharon. *Train Your Mind, Change Your Brain.* New York: Ballantine Books, 2007. 74-109.
13. Eliot, Lise, Ph.D. *What's Going on in There? How the Brain and Mind Develop in the First Five Years of Life* New York: Bantam Books, 2000. 354.

CHAPTER FIVE
Sensitive Periods Build Intelligence

1. Donald, Merlin, Ph.D. *Origins of the Modern Mind: Three Stages in the Evolution of Culture and Cognition.* Cambridge, MA: Harvard University Press, 1993. 199.
2. Bickerton, Derek, Ph.D. *Language and Species.* Chicago: University of Chicago Press, 1990. 77.

CHAPTER SIX
Conquering Everest

1. Montessori, Maria, MD. *The Absorbent Mind.* Amsterdam: Montessori-Pierson Publishing Company, 2007. 67-68.
2. Eliot, Lise, Ph.D. *What's Going on in There? How the Brain and Mind Develop in the First Five Years of Life.* New York: Bantam Books, 2000. 271.
3. Wilson, Frank R. *The Hand: How Its Use Shapes the Brain, Language, and Human Culture.* New York: Pantheon Books. 1998. 99.
4. Ibid. p. 97.
5. Ibid. p. 98.
6. Montessori, Maria, MD. *The Absorbent Mind.* New York: Delta Books, 1967. 151.
7. Wilson, Frank R., opt. cit. p.113.

8. Montessori, Maria, MD. *The Discovery of the Child*. Oxford, England: Clio Press, 1997 (reprinted 2004.) 59.
9. Wilson, Frank R., opt. cit. p. 103.
10. Eliot, Lise, Ph.D. opt. cit. p. 277.
11. Montessori, Maria, MD. *Education for a New World*. Oxford, England: Clio Press. 1989. 54.

CHAPTER SEVEN
Talk, Talk, Talk

1. Eliot, Lise, Ph.D. *What's Going on in There? How the Brain and Mind Develop in the First Five Years of Life*. New York: Bantam Books, 2000. 354.
2. Ibid. p. 357.
3. Ibid. p. 359.
4. Ibid. p. 372.
5. Donald, Merlin, Ph.D. *Origins of the Modern Mind: Three Stages in the Evolution of Culture and Cognition*. Cambridge, MA: Harvard University Press, 1993. 201.
6. Wilson, Frank R., MD. *The Hand: How Its Use Shapes the Brain, Language, and Human Culture*. New York: Pantheon Books. 1998. 37.
7. Bickerton, Derek, Ph.D. *Language and Species*. Chicago, IL. University of Chicago Press, 1990.
8. Eliot, Lise, Ph.D., opt. cit. p. 353.

CHAPER EIGHT
Learning Through the Senses

1. Montessori, Maria, MD. *The Secret of Childhood*. Hyderabad, India: Orient Longman. 2002. 123.
2. Eliot, Lise, Ph.D., *What's Going on in There? How the Brain and Mind Develop in the First Five Years of Life*. New York, NY: Bantam Books, 2000. 345.
3. Ibid. p. 348

CHAPTER ELEVEN
This Is My Montessori School

1. Montessori, Maria, MD. *The Discovery of the Child*. Notre Dame, IN. Fides Publishers, Inc. 1967. 83.

BIBLIOGRAPHY

Begley, Sharon, *Train Your Mind, Change Your Brain*, Ballantine Books, New York, NY, 2007.

Bickerton, Derek, *Language and Species*, University of Chicago Press, Chicago, IL, 1990.

Bronowski, Jacob, *The Origins of Knowledge and Imagination*, Yale University Press, New Haven, CT, 1978.

Donald, Merlin, *Origins of the Modern Mind: Three Stages in the Evolution of Culture and Cognition*, Harvard University Press, Cambridge, MA, 1993.

Eliot, Lise, *What's Going on in There? How the Brain and Mind Develop in the First Five Years of Life*, Bantam Books, New York, NY, 2000.

Erikson, Erik H. *Childhood and Society*, W.W. Norton&Company, Inc. New York, NY, 1963.

Greenfield, Susan A., *BBC Brain Story: Unlocking Our Inner World of Emotions, Memories, Ideas and Desires*. BBC Worldwide Limited, London, England, 2000.

Montanaro, Sivana Quattrocchi, *Understanding the Human Being: The Importance of the First Three Years of Life*, Nienhuis Montessori USA, Mountain View, CA. 1991.

Montessori, Maria, MD. *Education for a New World*, Clio Press, Oxford, England, 1999.

Montessori, Maria, MD. *Spontaneous Activity in Education*, Schocken Books, New York, NY, 1969.

Montessori, Maria, MD. *The Absorbent Mind*, Delta Books, New York, NY, 1967.

Montessori, Maria, MD. *The Discovery of the Child*, Fides Publishers, Inc., Notre Dame, IN, 1967.

Montessori, Maria, MD. *The Discovery of the Child*, Clio Press, Oxford, England, 1997 (reprinted in 2004).

Montessori, Maria, MD. *The Secret of Childhood*, Fides Publishers, Inc., Notre Dame, IN, 1970.

Montessori Maria, MD. unpublished London Lectures, 1946.

Montessori, Maria, MD. "The Need for Universal Accord So That Man May Be Morally Trained to Defend Humanity," *AMI Communications*, No. 4, 2001

Montessori, Maria, MD. *Formation of Man*, Clio Press, Oxford, England, 1989.

Montessori, Mario, Jr., *Education for Human Development*, Schocken Books, New York, NY, 1977.

Pearce, Joseph Chilton, *The Biology of Transcendence: A Blueprint of the Human Spirit*, Park Street Press, Rochester, VT, 2002.

Shore, Rima, *Rethinking the Brain: New Insight into Early Development*. Families and Work Institute, New York, NY, 1997.

Standing, E.M., *Maria Montessori: Her Life and Work*, Penguin Putnam, Inc., New York, NY,1984.

Wilson, Frank R., *The Hand: How Its Use Shapes the Brain, Language, and Human Culture*, Pantheon Books, New York, NY, 1998.

INDEX

Note that page numbers in bold indicate an illustration or diagram.

STUDY GUIDE

CHAPTER ONE
The Century of the Child

1. What influences greatly impacted Dr. Maria Montessori's life, both professionally and personally?

2. In what ways did Dr. Montessori's work become a worldwide movement?

   Activity: Think of one challenge that Dr. Montessori faced in her life. How would you have handled that situation?

CHAPTER TWO
The Relevance of Montessori in Modern Times

1. Is Dr. Montessori's work still relevant in today's modern world? If so, in what ways?

2. Can we use modern research to justify Montessori education?

CHAPTER THREE
The Big Picture of Child Development

1. What are the advantages/limitations of a stage-theory approach to explaining aspects of child development?

2. What aspects of development in the third plane (adolescence) are similar to aspects of the first plane (0-6 years)?

   Activity: Think about aspects of your own personality. Which planes of development were instrumental in forming these aspects?

CHAPTER FOUR
The Child's Mind

1. In what ways is the mind of a young child up to age six different from an adult mind?

2. How can you support a child's absorbent mind?

CHAPTER FIVE
Sensitive Periods for Building Intelligence

1. How can you see evidence of sensitive periods in the life of a child?

2. What significant aspects of child development are most influenced by sensitive periods?

3. Are there subtle aspects of development influenced by sensitive periods that are not as observable as others?

   Activity: Write a description of your earliest memory in life. Underline all the words that represent memories related to your senses (touch, smell, taste, sight, and hearing).

Chapter Six
Conquering Everest

1. In what way does the development of movement reflect a child's developing brain?

2. Does Dr. Montessori's outline of the development of movement still ring true today?

3. What current social/cultural influences can have a great impact on the development of movement?

4. How can parents support the natural development of movement in their children?

   Activity: Attempt to eat one meal with a large serving spoon and serving fork to experience what it's like for children living in an environment that is totally adult sized. Or look at your home environment and list any obvious obstacles to movement, especially for a young child.

Chapter Seven
Talk, Talk, Talk

1. What are simple ways to support the development of a good vocabulary in a child?

2. Vocabulary is built upon life experiences. What sorts of experiences can you provide for children without "teaching" them in a traditional manner?

3. How important is it to have spontaneous conversations with children every day?

   Activity: Listen to a child's spontaneous conversations (most of these will be with themselves!) and make a list of five of the child's current interests. Then, sit down and have a conversation with the child around one of these interests.

Chapter Eight
Learning Through the Senses

1. A child builds categories/classifications and catalogs of sensory data from experience. How can you support this natural ability in a young child?

2. Sensory overload is common in today's world. How can you protect a child from this overwhelming experience?

Chapter Nine
From Chaos to Order

1. Order is an essential aspect in a child's development. How can you provide external order without becoming rigid and inflexible?

2. What aspects of building order in a child's mind can be supported through the home environment?

   Activity: Think of your routine when you get up in the morning and get ready for your day. Do you do the same tasks in the same order every day? How important is this routine to getting a good start to your day?

Chapter Ten
This Is My Family and My Home

1. Home is a child's safe haven. Are you providing this physical and psychological haven for children in your life?

2. What are three simple things you can do at home to better support the natural development of children in your life?

CHAPTER ELEVEN
This Is My Montessori School

1. What advantages are offered to a child through a Montessori experience?

2. How can you keep realistic expectations about children and their Montessori school?

Activity: Think of your own early school experiences. How different are they from children in your life who attend a Montessori school?

About the Author

Jo De Banzie, London

M. SHANNON HELFRICH is an AMI *(Association Montessori Internationale)* teacher trainer, examiner and consultant. Most recently, she trained Montessori teachers at the International Training Center of Montessori Education of China in Hangzhou, China from 2007 through 2011. Shannon has been an AMI Montessori teacher since 1972. She worked in Montessori Children's House classrooms in Chicago, Illinois and Milwaukee, Wisconsin. She then founded two Montessori schools, one in Bismarck, North Dakota and the other in Gresham, Oregon.

In 1989, Shannon completed the AMI Training of Trainers program and was appointed the Director of Training at the Montessori Education Center of Oregon, which soon became the Montessori Institute Northwest. Since then, she has also directed courses at the Australia Montessori Teacher Education Foundation, helped found a training center in western Bangkok, Thailand and trained teachers in Hangzhou, China. Shannon is based in Tucson, Arizona, and lectures throughout the United States and internationally on Montessori education. This is her first book. Visit her web site at www.shannonhelfrich.com and email her at shannon@shannonhelfrich.com.